Montague George Jessett

The Key to South Africa: Delagoa Bay

Montague George Jessett

The Key to South Africa: Delagoa Bay

ISBN/EAN: 9783744751162

Printed in Europe, USA, Canada, Australia, Japan

Cover: Foto ©Andreas Hilbeck / pixelio.de

More available books at **www.hansebooks.com**

Photo by: RIGHT HON. C. J. RHODES. Elliot & Fry

THE KEY TO
SOUTH AFRICA:
DELAGOA BAY

BY
MONTAGUE GEORGE JESSETT, F.R.G.S.

WITH MAPS AND ILLUSTRATIONS

LONDON
T. FISHER UNWIN
PATERNOSTER SQUARE
MDCCCXCIX

CONTENTS

	PAGE
INTRODUCTION	xi

CHAPTER I
EARLY HISTORY 1

CHAPTER II
LOURENÇO MARQUES AND DELAGOA BAY . . 13

CHAPTER III
LOURENÇO MARQUES AND DELAGOA BAY (*continued*) 52

CHAPTER IV
THE NATIVES, FAUNA AND FLORA, ETC. . . 87

CHAPTER V
THE DELAGOA BAY AND NETHERLANDS RAILWAYS . 110

CHAPTER VI
THE TRADE, ETC., OF DELAGOA BAY . . . 133

CHAPTER VII
POLITICAL HISTORY 159

LIST OF ILLUSTRATIONS

THE RIGHT HON. C. J. RHODES . . *Frontispiece*

	PAGE
VASCO DA GAMA	11
LIGHTHOUSE AT REUBEN POINT . . .	15
KIOSQUE IN THE SQUARE, LOURENÇO MARQUES .	23
LOURENÇO MARQUES, VIEW FROM THE HILL ABOVE THE TOWN	39
MAP OF DELAGOA BAY	45
GENERAL VIEW OF LOURENÇO MARQUES . .	59
GARDENS NEAR THE CUSTOM HOUSE . . .	69
ROAD LEADING FROM DELAGOA BAY . . .	79
THIN-BRANCHED EUPHORBIA	103
MAP OF THE DELAGOA RAILWAY . . .	111
A STATION ON THE DELAGOA RAILWAY . .	129

"Lord God of Hosts, be with us yet!
Lest we Forget! Lest we Forget!!"

"*The Recessional*," KIPLING.

INTRODUCTION

It is with great diffidence that I submit the following pages for the perusal of the public. In them I have sought to throw a little light on the subject of our position respecting Delagoa Bay so far as regards foreign powers; to give a short history of the port, with an account of its trade, &c.; a brief account of the natives, and the fauna, flora, &c.; a *resumé* of the facts relating to the Delagoa Bay Railway dispute and the subsequent arbitration proceedings; and some slight account of the harbour, its town of Lourenço Marques, and the surrounding country.

INTRODUCTION

In view of the projected acquisition of Delagoa Bay by Great Britain, the greatest interest must be aroused in what should quickly prove to be one of our most valued possessions.

It is of the highest value both from a commercial and a strategical point of view. In brief, it is the key to South Africa, and means much more to us than the mere acquisition of further territory, for it ensures to us our proud position as the paramount Power in South Africa, and is a most important factor in the maintenance of peace.

Looking at the strained relationship that has unfortunately existed for so long past between Great Britain and the Transvaal Republic, it has become absolutely necessary to our safety that the Bay should not fall into hostile hands.

After many years of scheming on the part of other powers, our own diplomacy is, we hope and believe, to be rewarded, and this, our latest possession, will shine as one of the brightest jewels in the Crown of the Empire.

By every Imperialist this acquisition must be hailed with delight, and by it the hearts of all true Englishmen will be gladdened, for the best interests of our country and our colonies will be furthered, the integrity of our Empire assured, and a guarantee of peace obtained.

It is therefore only natural that every Briton should seek to know something of our latest acquisition, and my endeavour has been to give a rough and general outline of the place and our position respecting it.

When in South Africa, I had the honour of visiting that grand Imperialist and great Englishman, Mr. Rhodes—a man who, by his keen insight and cheery, undaunted optimism, has laid the foundation of that great wave of Imperialism—an Imperialism stronger, more appealing than that of the late Lord Tennyson and of the eminent

INTRODUCTION

Rudyard Kipling—which has spread itself throughout the country, nay, throughout the world, as evidenced by Germany's ceaseless desire for Colonial expansion. I then obtained such an insight into his glorious work for the advancement of his fellow-creatures and the honour and glory of his beloved land, that I was imbued with a strong desire to become acquainted with the policy of our Government respecting our splendid possessions in South Africa, and to gain all the information that I could regarding the colonies and the aims and politics of the people.

Particularly did I feel interested in the magnificent possibilities of the natural harbour of Delagoa Bay, where Mr. Rhodes has for long worked hard to acquire an interest both in the Bay and in the Railway, and his efforts in this direction need no further comment here at my hands.

Having devoured all the literature appertaining to the subject that was obtainable,

INTRODUCTION

I formed the resolution of visiting the place and seeing for myself whether the harbour really deserved the eulogistic accounts that I had read. The result was an absolute confirmation, for I found that it was quite as fine as it was painted, and in reality surpassed my most sanguine expectations. The size, the grandeur, the natural conformation, and the unique position were proved at once. The harbour was full of shipping, including some obsolete types of vessels belonging to the Portuguese Navy. *En passant*, in glaring contrast, at the entrance to the harbour was moored H.M.S. *Fox*, which quite accorded with my idea of the fitness of things.

At this time, viz., in 1897, there were no rumours of the possible acquisition of the Bay by England, either on lease or otherwise, but I felt, for all that, that we had a very strong right there, owing to the terms of the treaty entered into between England and Portugal, by which we were given the

INTRODUCTION

absolute right of pre-emption, and also considering our claims on Portugal and her indebtedness to us.

When at Delagoa Bay I consequently carefully studied the place and its surroundings, also its history and the political situation, and the result of my labours I now put before my readers, with the hope that they may derive some useful information therefrom, and will accord my efforts every indulgence when they consider the object of my task, which has only been to provide some general information in a concise form, and so save them from the necessity of having to wade through larger volumes dealing only scantily and incidentally with the various portions of this subject. I have further sought to emphasise the fact, that should we obtain possession of the Bay, it will open up a magnificent field for the energy and enterprise of our fellow-countrymen, who should not be slow in availing themselves of its advantages.

INTRODUCTION

My best thanks are due to Mr. E. P. Mathers for the loan of some of the illustrations which have appeared in his excellent paper, *South Africa,* from which I have derived much useful and interesting information.

Some of the facts relating to the earlier history of Delagoa Bay I have culled from Mr. McCall Theals' entertaining work entitled "The Portuguese in South Africa."

I have been at some pains to collect the various accounts given by travellers and residents, which are inserted in this book, my object being to set forth the views and opinions of all classes, and should it be considered that my strictures on the Portuguese and their methods have been too severe, a careful perusal of these accounts will, I think, amply justify my remarks and the conclusions I have come to.

M. G. J.

ENFIELD, *July,* 1899.

CHAPTER I

EARLY HISTORY

THE Portuguese—those grand old adventurers—were the early pioneers of exploration of new and far-distant lands. To their hardihood, their enterprise, and their insatiable love for exploration, we are indebted for many of the early discoveries that were made. Had it not been for them, these new countries would doubtless have remained *terræ incognitæ* until a very much later period. Those were the days when Portugal had a right to be proud of her sons, and justly reckoned herself a power in the world. To one of these hardy adventurers, viz., Vasco da Gama, is due the honour of first discovering Delagoa Bay. On the 4th of July, 1497, the famous Portuguese navigator sailed from Lisbon in command of three vessels, bent on discovering a new route to India by rounding the Cape of Good Hope. After a long and adventurous voyage, he sailed along the shores of that country which he appropriately named "Natal," as he first saw it on Christmas Day. Proceeding along the south-east coast, he discovered Delagoa Bay, where he met with a good reception at the hands of the natives, and then explored the east coast from Quillimane to Beira and Mozambique. For his services he was created a count and made Admiral of the Persian, Indian, and Arabian Seas.

In January, 1502, he made another voyage, this time being in command of twenty vessels. One of these ships, under the command of Antonio do Campo, lost the rest of the fleet and got disabled near Cabo das Correntes, and in this condition simply drifted until she fortunately got shelter in a large bay, which they called the "Bahia da Lagoa," or Bay of the Lake. The natives were very kind to Do Campo and his crew, and treated them well in every respect. They gained a lot of knowledge about the place, and found that three different rivers, called respectively the Maniça, the Espirito Santo, and the Maputa, flowed into the bay. He died in India on the 24th December, 1525.

The famous poem of Camoëns, "The Lusiad," is founded upon Da Gama's first discovery. The Portuguese have erected a monument to his memory at Beira. In May, 1898, great celebrations were held, both by Portugal and Great Britain, to celebrate the four hundredth anniversary of Da Gama's famous discoveries. In England the Royal Geographical Society held a special meeting, at which, conspicuous amongst a most brilliant assemblage, was the Prince of Wales, who, in the course of an excellent speech, said that England had every reason to be grateful to the Portuguese, because she had profited more than any other nation by their great discovery.

In 1505 a fleet of six ships, under the command of Pedro da Nhaya, sailed from Lisbon with the object of taking possession of Sofala. One vessel, losing the rest of the fleet, got into difficulties and put into Delagoa Bay. The captain, João de Queiros, and a portion of the crew, landed for the purpose of getting provisions, when they were attacked by the natives and most of them killed. Their ship was afterwards luckily picked up by one of the other vessels of the expedition, but only a few of the party were saved.

The Portuguese steadily continued their bold and adventurous voyages of discovery, but unfortunately they became gradually tinged with an inordinate desire for riches. In the year 1544 two Portuguese, named respectively Lourenço Marques and Antonio Caldeira, were sent on a voyage of exploration by the Captain of the Province of Mozambique. They embarked in a small and fragile vessel of the Arabian type, the narrow planks of which were sewed together, and was known as a "pangaio." In this frail concern they journeyed to the south, and after exploring the lower reaches of the Limpopo, and then the Espirito Santo, they went some distance up the Umbelosi, a tributary of the Espirito Santo. Subsequently they examined the Maputa river, where they got on very friendly terms with the chief and with the natives.

After this visit the Umbelosi river was called by the Portuguese the "Rio de Lourenço Marques," in the same way that the bay, which was formerly known as the Bahia da Lagoa, was called by them the "Bahia de Lourenço Marques." When the small village on the banks of the river was formed it naturally took the name of Lourenço Marques, although the bay itself remained known to all by its original name of Delagoa Bay, which it has ever since borne. After this a small trade in ivory, &c., was carried on between Lourenço Marques and Mozambique. A fair amount of tusks was brought down to the coast by the natives and taken across to Inyack Island, where they were stored until the traders picked them up.

A similar trade was carried on with Inhambane (a capital port about 230 miles further up the coast, and which provided good and safe anchorage), and also with Tete and Send, two trading stations on the Zambesi.

In the sixteenth century much was done by missionaries both in instructing the native tribes along the coast and in obtaining knowledge of them and of the country. One or two shipwrecks that took place also allowed the survivors to gain a good deal of information about the land and the people. A large galleon, named the *S. João*, was wrecked in 1552 near the mouth of the Umtamvuna river, and only a small proportion of the original passengers and crew were saved. These survivors, weak and almost exhausted as they were, set out for Lourenço Marques by walking along the shore, in the hope that they might come across some of the party who regularly traded between that place and Mozambique. It took these poor people over three months to reach the Umfusi river, which is one of the rivers flowing into Delagoa Bay. Their party was very much reduced, as they had lost many on the way through the terrible privations and sufferings that they had to endure. After a short stay, during which time they were very well treated by the natives, they made another start and crossed the Maputa river, only to fall into the hands of a treacherous native tribe, who robbed them of nearly all their belongings, including their clothes, and but very few of the whole party were ultimately saved. In 1589 another vessel, named the *S. Thomé*, was wrecked off the coast of Natal, and a certain number of the people on board took to the boats and succeeded in reaching Elephant Island, which is on the eastern side of Delagoa Bay. They landed and occupied the deserted huts of the traders, but they lost their boat by fire, and large numbers died from fever before the party were rescued and taken across to the mainland by the natives.

Various other shipwrecks occurred at different times off this coast, but otherwise Delagoa Bay was let severely alone. At this time there was no sufficient inducement for vessels to call there, as there was little or no trade to be done, the surrounding country and the hinterland not having been opened up at all.

For a very long period all this country remained in a practically stationary condition, and little was done either to improve the miserable little village of Lourenço

Marques, or to take advantage of the splendid harbour of Delagoa Bay. This was of course mainly to be accounted for by the fact that there was not much communication with the interior and consequently very little trade to be done. After 1752, the separation of the East African Government from that of Goa was effected by royal decree and a governor was appointed having his residence at Mozambique. All the other officials, from Lourenço Marques to Cape Delgado, were put under his charge and were accountable to him. In 1763 took place the first introduction of municipal institutions in the various small settlements along the coast, although it was really a farce.

In 1856 a "junta" or council, composed of thirteen members, was formed at Mozambique, having sway over the whole of the province. Lourenço Marques was represented, and returned one member.

The Boer farmers and others seeing what splendid agricultural and grazing land there was to the north of the Vaal river had trekked there from Cape Colony and formed various settlements. This of course at once brought Delagoa Bay to the front, as it is the nearest port and the natural outlet of the Transvaal; still, owing to there being no road or proper means of communication with the port, affairs at the bay did not progress very rapidly.

Some of the names originally given to the various rivers flowing into the bay had been altered from time to time. The Espirito Santo is now called the English river. The Maniça was changed into the King George's river, although the old name is now used when reference is made to the lower portion of the river, the upper course being called the Komati. The old Rio da Lagoa, or Rio de Lourenço Marques, is now known by its Kafir name of the Umbelosi.

It was not until the construction of the Delagoa Bay Railway was commenced that any serious attempt was made to improve the harbour and extend the town of Lourenço Marques, and even then it has, until within the last few years, progressed but at a snail's pace.

Now it has a glorious future before it,

and with English grit and energy, backed up by English capital, the town and port will flourish and extend with a rapidity that is exactly in the inverse ratio to its former lethargic movements, and will quickly become one of our most valued possessions in South Africa.

VASCO DA GAMA.
Reproduced by permission from "South Africa"

CHAPTER II

LOURENÇO MARQUES AND DELAGOA BAY

DELAGOA BAY, which may rightly be described as the finest natural harbour in Africa, extends from 25° 20′ to 26° 30′ S. latitude, and has a length of nearly 70 miles from north to south and a width varying from 16 to 25 miles. It forms the southern extremity of the Portuguese territory of Mozambique. To the south of the bay is a long strip of land termed the Inyack Peninsula; running northward and in continuation are a number of shoals called respectively the Cutfield, the Dommett, the Hope, and the Cockburn, and also a reef known as the Lech Reef. Beyond the Cockburn is a large island termed Inyack Island and beyond it a smaller one called Elephant Island. The Cutfield has $2\frac{1}{4}$ fathoms, the Dommett and the Hope three fathoms each, and the Cockburn only one fathom at low water of spring tides.

The harbour is truly a magnificent one, and offers a safe anchorage for vessels of practically any tonnage. Nearly all the South African ports suffer from the disadvantage of having a sand bar, and Delagoa Bay is no exception, although it is not a serious consideration in this case, as there are navigable channels of good depth. The bar is nearly half a mile in width, and even at low water some 14 feet are registered.

From the bay to the inner harbour there is a fine sweep of water, making a magnificent approach to Lourenço Marques, which is situated on the left bank of the English river just below Reuben Point. Lourenço Marques is 25° 53′ S. and 32° 30′ E., and is about 7,000 miles from Southampton. The town is built upon a low-lying spit of sand, and is about as ill-chosen a site as could have been pitched upon. Proper drainage and the reclamation of the swamp at the back of the town have done much to improve matters; still, this site should not

have been originally selected. Reuben Point, however, is everything that could be desired in the shape of a residential locality, and is a harbour of refuge to those suffering from malarial fever or who are sick and debilitated.

Inyack Island, which lies at the mouth of the bay, is fairly large, and has a sandy soil covered with low-growing scrub. On the bluff, called Reuben Point, and occupying a splendid position, is the lighthouse, while beyond are the signal station and the barracks. Another lighthouse has recently been erected on the Cockburn Shoal by a French company, which will prove of material advantage. The entrance to the inner harbour is by no means difficult, as the navigable channels are fairly wide and deep and are plentifully supplied with buoys and marks. It is incumbent upon all merchant vessels, however, to take a Government pilot aboard.

The water deepens in the fairway as the English river is approached—but shoals on the further side from Lourenço Marques—and varies somewhat in depth in different parts; as much as ten fathoms are registered just beyond the town.

The anchorage is good and the holding safe, as the harbour is so well sheltered. The length of the inner harbour is about seven miles and varies greatly in width, the widest part being about two miles. The Matola, the Umbelosi, and the Tembe rivers flow into the harbour, the two latter being good sized rivers and navigable for some distance. Large sized vessels can get a fairish way up, and lighters can proceed for many miles further.

The view of the bay, as seen from Lourenço Marques, is really superb. It is such a magnificent expanse of water that it well repays one to climb the hill and gaze upon it under the varying conditions of early morn, with the rising sun just tinting the distant sea with soft colours; broad day, with the glorious effulgence on the rippling waves; evening, with the setting sun showing weird effects by the depth and multiplicity of the colours cast upon the waters; and lastly night, when all is still and peaceful, and the sea is bathed in the liquid light of the moon.

The shores of the bay are rather low and in parts swampy, though near the town much has been done to remedy this state of things, due to the initiative of Governor Castilho, who flourished many years ago.

The town of Lourenço Marques, as viewed from the harbour, is without doubt extremely picturesque, owing partly to the undulating nature of the land and partly to the complete absence of any uniformity in the buildings. The town is built on loose sandy soil, which makes walking somewhat trying where the roads have not been made up, consequently 'rickshas and other vehicles are much in favour with the inhabitants. On a hot, dusty day it is rather a trying climb up the hill to Reuben Point, but, as before remarked, it is well worth the trouble on account of the splendid view to be obtained. A recently written account says that "it is not until the visitor gets on to the hill and has one of the most magnificent panoramas in the world at his feet, that he sees what Lourenço Marques is really like and what its destiny must be. The hill is to Lourenço Marques what the beautiful

Berea is to Durban in Natal. There is not the wealth of forest and of flowers here as at the Berea ; but there are residences as fine, and building is going on apace. It is said that the hill as a residential suburb of Lourenço Marques is substantially of only three years' growth. It is marvellous. The tasteful designs of the newly laid out gardens indicate what the hill will be like in a few years, and the way in which flowers grow in the open would provoke the envy of the Veitches and other floriculturists of England. And the view from the residences!

"A broad ribbon of blue water, much over a mile in width, coming down from the mountains, is faintly seen through the haze of distance, and joining the waters of the Indian Ocean as they surge in and out of Delagoa Bay, which stretches before one's view, lake-like and of vast expanse."

It is easy to predict that with British energy, British capital, and British go-ahead ideas the hill will before long become a really beautiful residential locality boasting fine houses, well planted avenues of trees, good macadam roads, which are badly wanted, and a tramway running along the Estrada da Punta Vermelha, leading to Reuben Point. On the top of the hill the air is good and invigorating, and the olfactory organs are unassailed by noxious effluvia. Some years ago Lourenço Marques had a most unenviable reputation as a hotbed of malarial fever. This was principally due to the swamp down by the river, which is happily a thing of the past. The sanitation formerly was simply horrible—even latterly it left much to be desired; but now it is distinctly improved and will, without doubt, shortly be perfected in every way.

There is now an excellent water supply, which is, particularly in tropical or semi-tropical climes, a matter of the utmost importance. There are public fountains, shady kiosks, fine trees, and luxuriant vegetation, so that it is easy to perceive that the town —which after all is only in an embryonic state—should shortly become a flourishing commercial port and a well-built and picturesque residential town.

The judicious planting of trees will do

much, not only to beautify the place, but to improve the sanitary conditions.

There have recently been established botanic gardens, which are really excellent. They are well laid out, and after they have had an opportunity of becoming set, with care and attention they should prove a most valuable addition to the town and a popular place of public resort. Trees, shrubs, and plants alike seem to flourish in a truly wonderful manner, so there is no reason why these gardens should not eventually favourably compare with those at Cape Town, Durban, Johannesburg, &c. Public gardens are a boon to any South African town, and during the hot months are a real want and an undisguised blessing. Lourenço Marques is a truly cosmopolitan town, and it is quite a liberal education to study the various types of the genus *homo* (representatives of many different nationalities) to be found here. English, French, Germans, Portuguese, Arabs, Chinese, Japanese, Indians, and Kafirs all jostle one another down by the docks, in the streets, and about the squares. As the population is

KIOSQUE IN THE SQUARE, LOURENÇO MARQUES.
Sketched by the Author.

varied so are the character and nationality of the buildings. Here is a well-built residence of European architecture, there a mosque with oriental minarets, beyond a gaudy-painted Arab store, and next to it an up-to-date café or restaurant. Some of the buildings are of a very good and substantial character and built in accordance with the requirements of the locality and the climate. The coloured population is a fairly large one, and, besides the natives, consists of a good proportion of Indians and Banyans.

The Indians seem to get everywhere, but there is no doubt that they are a hard-working and thrifty race, and wherever they go they manage to thrive and multiply. There is something to be said in their favour, for their work, which benefits them so largely, has also a resultant effect upon the community. They have most certainly more enterprise, more perseverance, and more business aptitude than any of the native African races, and consequently they must do some good to their particular localities, and by their example and the competition they engender stimulate the dormant energies and faculties of the natives. Most of the small native trading stores at Lourenço Marques are in the hands of the Indians, Banyans (or Arabs), Chinese, and Japanese, who manage to make very good livings and prosper exceedingly.

The town extends just over a mile along the bay, and is picturesquely situated. A lot of the reclaimed land, which was formerly swamp, now forms good wharfage. Much has been done recently to improve the harbour, docks, landing-stages, &c., but still it has been done slowly and in Portuguese style. Now, however, vast improvements and colossal alterations and additions will, without doubt, quickly be made, and the whole place will soon be transmogrified and put upon a proper footing, as is the due of such an important and magnificent harbour. Then an immense trade will quickly be attracted to the port, and the town and the harbour and surroundings will increase and flourish accordingly. With the advent of electric trams, and the other benefits conferred by electricity, in addition to the electric light installation it now enjoys,

Lourenço Marques will awake from her lethargy and will take her rightful place among the flourishing towns of South Africa.

For many years past Lourenço Marques has been a disgrace to any European nation, and its magnificent and unrivalled advantages as a port have never properly been taken advantage of by the Portuguese. The terrible way in which goods were delayed in transport, the state of chaos which prevailed, and the horrible abuses in the Custom House at Lourenço Marques are best described in the following article, which appeared in a *Portuguese* newspaper, called the *Diario do Commercio*, published in Funchal, in Madeira, No. 1,318, of 22nd March, 1896, the translation of which appeared in the columns of *South Africa:*—

" We beg leave to transcribe from the *Jornal do Commercio* of Lisbon part of a correspondence sent to that valuable paper by one of our most distinct friends and a most honest official, residing in Lourenço Marques. That which is going to be read is a cry of indignation from the strict conscience of a perfectly honest man against that pack of fools (and we might say of bandits) to whom the government of this country is entrusted. With such government there is no valour or bravery that can raise a people from the degradations and abasements they are subjected to by their rulers. Our Western and Eastern Africa is plunging in every kind of corruption, and can only be saved from it by an energetic dose of morality and liberty employed abnormally in reforms made by the Government to colonial services. But who in Portugal expects anything useful from the men at the head of public affairs? It is not only in Africa that everything is demoralised. We have also here the same corruption and debasement presiding over every affair. The only question is to divide the ragged tunic of the country amongst half a dozen lackeys. Nothing else.

"The following is the part of the correspondence referred to :—

"'The same disorganisation still continues and will continue until the Government of the Mother Country resolves to send out here an Inspecting Committee, as it has done with other Custom Houses on the Western Coast. Such an inspection is not to be delayed. Here the service is much more disorganised than on the Western Coast. There you can find out the frauds, I assure you, as easily as in Lisbon, Oporto, and every other Custom House.

"'Here you cannot. They are known, they are seen, but nobody is enabled to inquire into them. The utmost confusion reigns, and it is an impossibility to describe it. An Inspecting Committee, composed of the Crown Attorney, the Chief of the Revenue Office, and the Book-keeper of the Banco Ultramarino, are inquiring into abuses and crimes, but the Committee does not organise the service, nor have they instructions to do so. The statistical maps only reach 1890! It is a service nobody executes, because there is nobody to execute it. The demoralised officials, most of them without any knowledge of Custom House service, fail continuously in their duty or are on leave! Consequently those who have a good will and are apt to work, being left in a small number, cannot do everything. There are no books of entry of merchandise and no store books! Indeed, they would be of no use, as the Custom House Guards are soldiers from the Police Corps, who can neither read nor write! The principal Custom House stores are—a large square without the slightest shelter, the pier, and the street. The collector wanted to finish with this state of things, and asked for store books, but God only knows if they ever will be supplied. He also gave orders that all goods should be put under shelter, and only large and heavy packages to be left in the square; but as such an order will not suit anybody, and as the collector was absent on account of being suspended, an order in writing was given— a thing never done before—to the sub-collector, who was then acting-collector, to allow all merchandise to be stowed away in the square. This was under the profligate Governor. There are still, at the time of writing, packages afloat in lighters of landing companies, taken away from the cargo steamers in November, and certificates have been given by the Custom House stating that such packages have not been landed at this port. Prestige and power were lessened to the collector, as it was not convenient he should have them so that only disorder and confusion might reign, and then that merchandise might only be cleared by those who could not help it. . . . The Custom House archives are in a room heaped on the ground; other documents are spread at random over the tables and in drawers and corners. The certificates are passed in a hoity-toity way, and it is not uncommon to hear people declaiming against the falsehoods of the certificates and proving them! Cases of petroleum, demijohns, &c., are landed, and in the night portions of them are taken home, and we say so, because there are firms who, having landed 200 or 300 packages, next day they are short of 70 or 80, and they condemn themselves. The packages were stolen, they say! If this may be called a Custom House, or anything like it, "let the monkeys bite me," as the Kafirs in the interior say when they swear.'

"And that it may not be said I exaggerate I transcribe from the report attached to decree No. 87 of the High Commissioner, Councillor Antonio Ennes, published in the *Boletim Official* of the Province No. 3, of January 31st last, the following :—

"'In the beach close to the Custom House pier merchandise of a difficult sale is piled up, and passengers only manage to enter the town by crossing labyrinths formed by heaps of cases and bales, jumping over rails, knocking themselves against waggons, and being overthrown by carriers! These carriers drop the packages where it is most convenient according to the orders received, as under Article 117 of the Customs Regulation the discharge and stowing away of packages in the Custom House must be executed by labourers paid by their employers. Everything which is said here we know has been officially reported, but no laws have been made to remedy the evil. And because later on the present collector may be called to account for these facts, he gave several orders to regulate and put the service in order, and for that reason he was praised by the Cape and Transvaal papers, but he met with a decided war by the influential people of the place, especially the Portuguese. And later on it may be said that the present collector lacked energy to repress the abuses, but before he was on duty for more than a month he was suspended for attempting to finish them, thus remaining without prestige and power to continue on the great deal there is to be done.'"

"The Custom House of Lourenço Marques is a sea Custom House of the utmost importance, and still it does not possess a single boat! And it is sad to remember the reason why its boats were taken away. The Custom House used to hire them sometimes, and occasionally they were cast ashore in order that certain employés could let theirs for the service! But this fact did not cause any suspicions; the evil was stopped in its progress at the beginning and the boats were taken away. So that, whatever may happen in the port, the soldiers watch on shore by sleeping in the night and by walking during the day. It is necessary that these things should be made known, so that the responsibility may be taken by those who ought to take it, and not by one who has newly arrived and who should not have it, and also who is disabled and restrained from remedying this state of things."

This statement, written by a Portuguese, clearly shows the shocking state of things that has prevailed for so long past at this unrivalled port. It has been a wilful throwing away of magnificent chances to the utter detriment of trade and good name. Yet notwithstanding this, trade and the shipping have increased steadily, principally from the fact that the position is a unique one and the harbour itself is, *facile princeps*, the finest natural harbour on the whole of the coast.

It was really the visit of the British squadron to Delagoa Bay in 1897 that first attracted universal attention to this wonderful harbour. The flagrant abuses, the terrible mismanagement, the crass ignorance of the officials, and the woful state of chaos that then existed were shown up to the light of day and published abroad. This awful state of things could hardly be realised by the average European, and, no doubt, was in many instances looked upon as a gross exaggeration put forward by designing persons to serve their own ends. A visit to Lourenço Marques, however, would have quickly served to disillusionise the most sceptical. Most of this was due to two prime causes, viz., the poverty-stricken state of the Portuguese and their confirmed dilatory, procrastinating natures.

The Cape papers recently contained some very severe criticisms on the Portuguese administration of Delagoa Bay, written by a traveller who had carefully studied the subject. He says: "At the Lourenço Marques railway station, the terminus of one of the finest trunk railways in Africa, connecting Johannesburg, Pretoria, and Barberton with the natural port of the Transvaal, there are no signals or semaphores of any description; a small brass trumpet answers instead. On the station platforms at the frontier and terminus some seats are placed, ostensibly for the convenience of the travelling public, but they are monopolised by the railway officials and soldiers, who, to all intents and purposes, act the part of sightseers. They all smoke cigarettes, lounge, and look fagged and worn out. Some twelve locomotives stood about in different conditions of rust, unprotected from the weather, evidently out of work. The sidings were full of empty trucks, waiting for loads which had been ordered to Durban, East London, and Port Elizabeth. The main, or Customs pier, where passengers and cargo are landed, I found was a splendid panorama for an observant man. Everything seemed at sixes and sevens. Portuguese soldiers, native men and women, Greek boatmen and fishermen, all seemed mixed up. The soldiers were the Customs clerks, marking each package with pots of red paint, the natives acting as carriers from the lighters to the Customs sheds, a waste of labour and time, to say nothing of the danger of breakage. The same thing is not to be seen in any other part of the world, at least under European control. An elderly gruff Englishman, with an immense sjambok in hand, who swore at every Kafir in choice Billingsgate, attracted my attention, and we exchanged "Good morning." He was engaged with a gang of natives in landing, preventing broaching, and "bossing" generally for the landing company. Presently a bell rang, and everybody left off work and disappeared. It was the Portuguese hour for breakfast, from ten to eleven o'clock. The gruff man sat down beside me and recounted some experiences. He told me about some supposed rotten potatoes in cases being thrown overboard from a lighter in midstream, which afterwards proved to be a consignment of Yöst typewriters. Like many other consignments landed at Delagoa Bay, this consignment cannot be accounted for since leaving the ship's side. He went on, pointing to a man searching amongst a huge heap of cases on the wharf: "That man," he said, "is a German from Johannesburg. Some time ago he imported 400 cases of tallow candles: he's still looking for them. I can tell you all about them. When landed they were left outside in the sun for months. You see that heap there covered with coal dust?

That's the tallow which melted and ran out of the cases. When the boxes were removed the bottoms fell out, and only the wicks were left. I'll bet he doesn't import any more German tallow candles through Delagoa Bay.'"

Innumerable instances of delay, neglect, wilful carelessness and crass ignorance could be cited, if enough had not already been said to show the woful state of things that exists at Delagoa Bay. It need hardly be said that the present Portuguese policy is a suicidal one. Owing to the want of proper piers and landing-stages, cargoes have to be transhipped into lighters and are then towed alongside the wharves. Instead of being immediately unladen and the freights duly despatched by rail, they would probably remain for a whole day unloaded; and then, when this operation was performed, the cargo would be dumped down anywhere and actually allowed to remain indefinitely, till it was either lost or spoilt.

The mind of the ordinary individual totally fails to grasp the state of things that used to prevail, for it is only quite recently that these conditions have been ameliorated in some slight degree. Cases of crockery and other fragile goods were hopelessly mixed up with barrels of cement, mining machinery and mining implements, and hosts of other goods, both of a perishable or flimsy nature and of a heavy, unyielding character. As a rule, of course, the light and easily breakable articles found their way down at the bottom and supported, or otherwise, huge packing-cases and ponderous barrels or crates. Not only did this chaotic state exist in the Customs shed and its vicinity, but goods were also dumped down in the public gardens and stacked there anyhow. This heterogeneous mass of valuable merchandise would lie for a lengthened period exposed to the elements, and would consequently get so inextricably mixed up that the consignee might account himself a lucky man if he ever get his goods at all, and luckier still if they arrived intact. The generality of the Portuguese officials in East Africa are bad in the extreme, corrupt, lazy, avaricious, and totally without conscience. They are the ne'er-do-wells whom the Government are only too glad to get rid of by giving them posts in their colonies. Their pay is extremely poor, yet they manage to keep up a good deal of style, and after a few short years retire to live in luxury and idleness. This forms food for speculation; for it is certain that the miserable pittances which represent the salaries drawn from the Government are not responsible for this state of things. After the visit of the British squadron, however, affairs began to mend a little. So many and such well-founded complaints were continually being made to the Government, that eventually some notice had to be taken of them, and Carlos the First, King of Portugal, addressed the Cortes of Lisbon, enjoining " some improvements for the better."

Undoubtedly marked improvements have been made in all directions. The jetties and wharves have been improved, cranes erected, and harbour works put in hand. The town of Lourenço Marques has made fair progress, although much still remains to be done. However, it is a step in the right direction, and not only does the place look cleaner and healthier, but there is more of a business appearance about the town, the wharves, and the harbour itself, which is a sure index that reforms have been made and that trade is gradually being attracted to the port. The Portuguese move slowly; how slowly, only those who have an intimate acquaintance with them and their methods can tell, and it was a subject for great congratulation to the inhabitants of Lourenço Marques to know that the Government had at last shaken off its apathy and was moving at all—more particularly that it was a step in the right direction and not a retrograde movement, which it might well have been.

If it has flourished, as it has to a limited degree, under Portuguese rule, what, then, must be its future condition when in English hands! Truly the place will be speedily altered and improved, and will quickly become a thriving, healthy, and busy port, working in harmony with all the other British ports, to the benefit of the Colony and the Mother Country.

From statistics published in *O Futuro*—a Portuguese paper—of the tonnage which entered the port of Delagoa Bay during the month of August, 1898, it shows an increase of 4,000 over the previous month. This looks distinctly well, and shows how, even in Portuguese hands, trade is bound to keep improving owing to the obvious advantages possessed by this port. At the present time there are as many as fifteen regular steamship lines calling at Lourenço Marques, and there is no doubt that with proper management and increased facilities in transit arrangements the shipping will be largely augmented. Of late years the Portuguese Government seems to have awakened, although tardily, to the fact that it has a harbour possessing not only the most wonderful natural advantages, but also a port that is in direct communication with the Transvaal and all the great goldfields. Consequently a good deal has been done towards establishing a fairly efficient service of pilots and properly lighting the port, so that vessels may get in during the night equally as well as in the daytime.

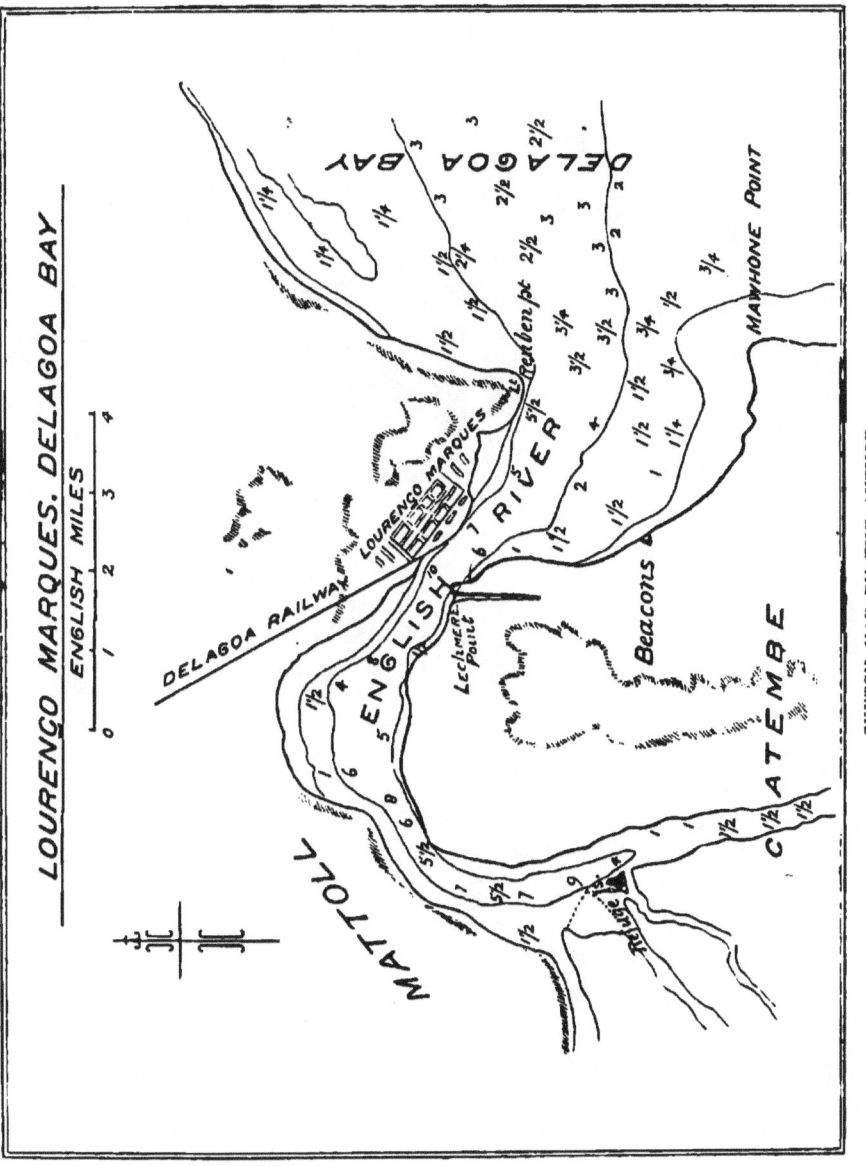

SKETCH MAP BY THE AUTHOR.

One writer, describing the port, remarks: "Several steamers enter the port now at night, and the health officials are always ready to meet vessels at the entrance of the river, and it is to be doubted whether on the south coast from the Cape to Durban a better *pratique* service is to be found. The town itself is a pleasant surprise to strangers who have never seen it, or even to those who have been absent for some time, such are the improvements to be seen everywhere; and there is no doubt, whether this port continues to be of Portuguese or any other nationality, the geographical position and manifest advantages cannot be taken from us. Thirty-five vessels, of which thirty-three were steamers, called here during August, 1898, and this alone in the bad times is very significant. I feel confident that not many months will elapse before a radical change will be experienced here; and if we are to give credence to the many rumours current about the rich finds of minerals along the Tembe and Umbelosi rivers, on the Lebombo Mountains and in Gazaland, together with the undoubtedly rich pasture and agricultural lands along the banks of the Maputo, Tembe, Umbelosi, and St. George rivers, I feel convinced that under a good government not only will the district be made a self-supporting one, but will show the world what its capabilities really are."

Another visitor to Delagoa Bay writes: "Along the river's edge was a stone embankment, from several parts of which piers projected. In the centre were two very large sheds belonging to the Customs House. Away to the right, high up the hill, was a square stone building with castellated spires at the corners—it was the powder magazine. In about the centre of the town stood a very pretty white church and near it a large hospital. Away to the left upon a projecting knoll were half a dozen large yellow barracks, and before them stood a saluting battery. At this extremity of the town were a railway station, machine shop, and car and locomotive sheds. Loaded trains were passing and added greatly to the European aspect of the place. I found it a very clean little town, with straight macadamised roads and concrete sidewalks. The dwellings and shops were mostly of one storey, two or three hotels were of two storeys. Most of the houses have iron roofs and sides. Upon one side of a neat square was the Governor's residence, an unpretentious building. You pass abruptly from the streets of the town to those running into the country, which are laid out with great width and bordered with rows of trees. The Botanic Garden, though small, is full of a great variety of trees belonging both to tropical and temperate zones. The town has considerable business activity. There are two or three hundred Europeans in business — Dutch, German, French, and English; the remainder of the population of some thousand inhabitants consists of Portuguese, Creoles, Banyans (or Arabs), and native Africans."

Since this was written the population has largely increased. According to the official census of the population at the end of December, 1897, there were 2,242 Europeans and Americans, 913 Asiatics, and 1,747 Africans, making a grand total of 4,902.

Since then the population has still further grown, the census for January, 1899, showing a total of 5,130, but in the near future there is every reason to believe that it will augment so rapidly that the town will soon grow out of all recollection of its present size and character. Lourenço Marques has now an excellent electric light installation, and can vie in this respect with any South African town. The concession is in the hands of a French company called the Compagnie Générale d'Electricité de Lourenço Marques, who will doubtless do extremely well out of this in the future.

Electric lighting is a great boon to a town, and particularly so to a port; and if Lourenço Marques only boasted electric tramways and telephones, the inhabitants would have great cause to congratulate themselves.

As before remarked, many of the roads consist merely of yielding red sand, which makes walking, especially in the heat, very trying. Some of the principal roads have been macadamised by the municipality, and these are very good indeed; but the Portuguese will take their time, and if left to themselves it would be many years before all the roads were made up.

They are totally incapable of producing lightning effects; thus the five or six miles of roads already finished have taken as many years to complete.

CHAPTER III

LOURENÇO MARQUES AND DELAGOA BAY

(Continued)

THE harbour at Delagoa Bay is really wonderful, owing to the natural configuration of the land. There is room for absolutely hundreds of vessels in the inner bay, and even at low water they can anchor fairly close in-shore.

If the proper works and harbour improvements were carried out (as they ought to have been years ago) vessels of any tonnage and draught should be able to come alongside the quays and wharves with perfect safety, and discharge their cargoes direct. The present system of employing lighters is not only expensive and troublesome, but also causes serious delay and often loss as well. When the harbour works are completed and proper arrangements made with regard to the railway, the traffic will be enormous. Consignors will quickly discover the vast difference implied in change of ownership, once we obtain possession.

At the present time the cost of living at Lourenço Marques is undoubtedly high, and its inhabitants suffer under many disadvantages, soon, we hope, to be removed. The taxes are heavy, and the climate at certain seasons of the year trying. However, for six or seven months in the year the climate is good, and the heat is not too great, more especially between the months of May and September. After the heat of the day deliciously cool breezes spring up each evening, coming direct from the sea, and instill new life and strength in the residents. At these periods of the year the nights are fairly cool and invigorating, and are very healthy and bearable for Europeans; after September, however, the climate is not so good, the heat during the daytime being very trying, and the moisture in the atmosphere, besides being unhealthy, induces a languor which is alike detrimental to business or sport. As a consequence there is a general exodus of those lucky ones whose means enable them to seek less trying and more invigorating localities. Formerly during this period malarial fever was rife owing to the swamps at the back of the town, but, although still prevalent, it is nothing like so virulent or general, owing to the filling-in of these swamps and the improved sanitation. It is stated that the death-rate during summer was at one time estimated at one-fifth of the population, but the percentage of deaths is now, comparatively speaking, very low, owing to the introduction of these sanitary improvements.

Undertakers may have flourished exceedingly in the past, but these worthies will not thrive so well in the future; they have had their "boom," and now the welcome "slump" in corpses has come, and the trade will never have a chance of regaining its pristine vigour. The Consular report for 1897 says: "The health of the town is improving year by year, and will soon compare favourably with that of Durban."

During the winter months both the evenings and the early mornings are particularly cold, and the contrast to the heat of the day, as shown by the thermometer, is very marked.

At times very high winds prevail, principally from the south-east. When it blows from the south the air is cool and refreshing, but a northerly wind is very trying and enervating and has the effect of scorching up everything.

Occasionally cyclones are experienced, which often cause a great deal of damage, as well as great interference with one's ordinary avocations.

Hailstorms and thunderstorms occur at intervals, and are usually rather violent, as in all tropical countries. Occasionally, particularly in the early morning, very thick mists arise, which blot out everything for the time being, but the rising sun, as a rule, quickly dispels them.

The constant reclamation of land that steadily goes on helps to make the town more healthy; in the neighbourhood of the Custom House between 20,000 and 30,000 square metres have been reclaimed from the sea, and this work is steadily progressing.

The town itself can hardly be called imposing, although it certainly looks very well, not to say picturesque, when viewed from the sea.

The principal avenues have wisely been constructed on wide lines. When England has control one may confidently expect to see fine rows of shops, with large plate-glass windows, displaying their wares—the bulk of which, let us hope, will be of British manufacture. There is a capital market in the town, where a large and curious assortment of edibles of all kinds may be seen. But particularly interesting are the strange products of the sea. Here one may see truly strange and weird marine specimens of the utmost interest to the visitor. Some of the native fish are of extraordinary shape, size, and colour, the native names of which are hardly less peculiar. Some have gorgeous colouring, rivalling the rainbow in the depth and multiplicity of their hues, others again have a dull leaden appearance which does not favourably impress one as to their being very desirable articles of diet. The various kinds of vegetables displayed for sale are also very interesting, particularly those of tropical growth.

The quay is a fairly broad one, and various streets lead from it. One of these, the Rua Guato y Castero, leads to the Plaza, and by any of these roads running from the quay the broad thoroughfare called the Avenida Don Carlos may be reached. All the streets and avenues are at right angles to each other, and are nearly all named after some particular individual.

Proceeding up the Avenida Aguiar the hospital is reached, a very fair building, and sometimes much in request. By turning to the right the long and straight Avenida Augusto de Castilho (named after a former governor) confronts one, and leads to the extreme back portion of the town. The wide avenue called the Avenida Central runs direct to the cemetery, which is fairly spacious and is situated immediately in the rear of the town.

THE KEY TO SOUTH AFRICA: DELAGOA BAY

By climbing the long hill, known as the Estrada da Punta Vermelha, the famous Reuben Point is reached. The road, which describes a semicircle at the Point, following the curve of the headland, is here called the Avenida da Marina. Fine residences and lovely gardens with beautiful flowers are to be seen at Punta Vermelha, which from its commanding and healthy situation forms a really grand residential quarter. A fine club-house has recently been built on the hillside at a cost of £25,000, which will doubtless prove a great boon to the residents. Reuben Point gets the full benefit of the refreshing and invigorating sea-breezes, which are felt here particularly after sundown, and, needless to say, they have a fine stimulating effect on those whose day has been spent in the lower quarters of the town.

The land in the rear of the residential quarter, which is of great extent, belongs to the East and South African Telegraph Company.

Two of the most imposing buildings in Lourenço Marques are the Roman Catholic

GENERAL VIEW OF LOURENÇO MARQUES.
Reproduced by permission from "South Africa."

church, situated about the centre of the town, and the " paiol," or powder magazine. This latter structure presents a decidedly picturesque appearance. Having a castellated top, and being built of large blocks of stone, it suggests more the appearance of a castle than a powder magazine. It occupies a fine commanding site on the hill.

The following account of the town was recently given by the Johannesburg *Star*: "The first thing that strikes one on arrival of the train at Lourenço Marques is the improvement which has taken place at the station. The electric light is a great improvement on the old oil lamp which formerly did service. Then there are some fine flower-beds laid out in front of the station, which give it quite a homely appearance.

"On emerging from the station one finds the main streets are all hardened—a great improvement on the sand which one's feet used to sink into in former days. Here we find a 'bus actually waiting to take travellers to the hotel at Reuben Point. Four-wheelers and 'rickshas are also on the stand for hire. Horsemen are to be seen in the street, and the New Woman on her bike may be noticed flying round a street corner.

"These are all signs of an advanced civilisation, even in this God-forsaken town. Very little improvement has taken place, however, in the buildings of the town. True, there are a few new ones bearing traces of having been recently put up; but, taken as a whole, the town has the same appearance which it had some ten years ago.

"This cannot be said, however, about the customs and shipping arrangements. Greatly improved facilities for unloading are now in full operation, seven steam cranes being in waiting to unload the lighters as they come forward. The Custom House is now covered in, with large sheds for the protection of goods. They are also enclosed with iron railings, which must prevent the great amount of thieving which used to take place, from the fact that the goods were simply dumped down in the sand and left to take care of themselves. Importers need not now fear any heavy loss being suffered under this head.

"The sanitary arrangements of the harbour are now greatly improved, a lavatory having been placed at the entrance to the jetty for the benefit of the public.

"Upon taking a walk through the town after sundown, one observes the change in the lighting of the streets, all of which are now well lit up with the electric light. The French company, which has got a concession, appears to be doing its work well, and has extended its operations right up to the end of Reuben Point.

"The company has got its works upon part of the space formerly occupied by the swamp, which does not appear to affect materially the health of those employed on the staff of the company. Touching on the swamp itself, I must say I was rather disappointed to see that very little work has been done to reclaim it during all those years. True, the water has been drained off, but very little of the swamp has been filled in. From all appearances the powers that be mean business, because I notice that all day long a locomotive is at work, with a long train of waggons, unloading soil into the swamp.

"The water supply now introduced into the town through water pipes must be a great blessing to the place. Apart from its value as drinking water, for washing and other domestic purposes it must be of great value to the community, and must go a great way towards improving the health of the town.

"There is no getting away from the fact that fever does exist here, but I do not consider it so very deadly after all, if proper precautions are taken, and care is observed in one's manner of living. Nobody can be surprised at some men dying here, if their mode of living is considered. Every one admits, however, that the fever is not now so bad as it was in former years, and it will continue to diminish just in proportion to the amount of attention the authorities devote to the sanitary improvement of the town. If this town was placed under the same sanitary condition as Durban, there is no reason why it should not be as healthy as that place. The town of Lourenço Marques itself is not healthy at present, and it will remain in this state just as long as the authorities allow the coloured population to live under present conditions. There appears to be a great deal of overcrowding of this portion of the population, and until this insanitary condition is obviated Delagoa Bay cannot possibly be healthy.

"The indiscriminate granting of licenses for the sale of liquor is another matter which requires the attention of the authorities. It appears that licenses are granted to all who apply, no matter of what colour the applicant may be, or what character he bears. The circumstances of the applicant are never inquired into, and the result is that all sorts and conditions obtain licenses, even down to the Chinaman.

"The European Bar is run by a Chinaman, and there appear to be no regulations regarding hours for the sale of liquor. The bars appear to be always open, on Sundays and weekdays alike. Chinamen sell liquor to natives at all times; and every one must admit that this is a dangerous practice, and not in the interest of the community at large to have numbers of natives moving about the streets at all hours of the night in a semi-intoxicated state.

"A number of 'ladies' are allowed to run something like half the bars in the town, and this is certainly a disgrace. The authorities who conduct the affairs of the town should certainly, if they must be allowed to remain in the town, at once remove them from the main streets. Their conduct is shameful, and they enjoy a freedom of action which would not be allowed anywhere else. Then, again, the business which they conduct affects the trade of the respectable bars, the result being a difficulty on the part of the latter to meet expenses.

"Practically speaking, there is no Sunday in Lourenço Marques. Trading goes on as usual, principally amongst the small tradesmen and the coloured storekeepers, who conduct more than half the local trade. The large European storekeepers, the forwarding agents, and the banks are all closed, but for all that a large amount of business is done on the Sabbath.

"On Sunday afternoon I took a walk to Reuben Point to have a look at the new township which has sprung up there during the last two years. I could scarcely believe my eyes, such a transformation had taken place. I found a good hard road, with the electric light fixed up right on to the Point. There must be at least fifty houses in occupation, while others are in course of erection. Some of them would hold their own against the villas of Doornfontein. Trees are being planted, flower-beds are laid out, and everything is done to make life pleasant and enjoyable. All the high Government officials, and all those who pretend to be anybody, live up at the Point.

"On walking along the road, greatly to my surprise, I met a few carriages containing gentlemen with the regulation black coat and tall hat, accompanied by ladies dressed in the latest fashion. I passed the cable station, and there I found a group of young men playing lawn tennis along with a young lady. She had all the young men to herself, and appeared to be enjoying herself greatly. This state of things will not continue long, however, for she will soon have rivals in the field, or I am very much mistaken. What there is to prevent people living a healthy life in a place like Reuben

Point I cannot tell. It is facing the open sea, and in the afternoon a beautiful sea-breeze comes blowing in, and where the fever can come from I do not know. Jim Carpenter, the old Barbertonian, has a grand hotel on the Point, fitted up with every convenience for travellers. It is well managed, and a 'bus runs to and from town morning and evening. Indeed, Reuben Point will become in time a health resort, and people from the Rand in search of a change will make for this place, instead of going to Sea Point (Cape Town) or the Berea (Durban).

"As regards the general life of the inhabitants, except as I have said, the few aristocrats referred to, who copy the European plan of *fin de siècle* existence, it is much the same as it was ten years ago. Blacks still monopolise the public thoroughfares, and both whites and blacks seem afraid of hard work; while all of them, irrespective of age or sex, appear to regard life as a mere long period of enjoyment, having no sorrows and no serious drawbacks. As in the tropics, the people mostly lead an out-

GARDENS NEAR THE CUSTOM HOUSE, LOURENÇO MARQUES, DELAGOA BAY.

door existence, and kiosks and cafés, after the style of the Boulevards in Paris, abound. There, of an evening, Delagoa Bay and his wife turn in to quaff the red wine and eat confectionery. This happy condition, however, is occasionally disturbed, especially at night time, by the freaks of the military. There are no actual police here, but the soldiers serve as police when required. These gentlemen very often, possibly from over-exuberant spirits, amuse themselves by firing off revolvers, and it is no surprising sight to see citizens running round the corners of the streets to dodge the bullets. This kind of pleasantry sometimes mars the evening's enjoyment, but, as the inhabitants have been accustomed to the practice for years, and as very few people have been shot in consequence, nobody minds it. As for making a fuss over such a paltry matter, the real Delagoa Bayians rather like the fun. 'Other times, other manners,' and the time will possibly come when firing ball cartridge in the streets will not be considered good form; but that is not yet. At present the soldiery feel that they need some stimulant to drive away *ennui;* and what is more bracing, more likely to make a really brave man feel his bravery than to use firearms, and, so to speak, see bullets flying from you rather than towards you? Perhaps it is some such idea which animates our local warriors. But this apart, the soldiers are not bad fellows, while the officers are both gentlemanly and courteous, and really enliven our little social circles.

"On the whole, there are many worse places than Delagoa Bay, and, as it is now making a strong bid for popularity as a port, and doing its best to make all up-to-date improvements required for that purpose, it cannot be doubted that in a few years it will not only have a much larger population than it has at present, but will also assume most of the characteristics of a civilised town."

Even since this account was written a fair amount of improvement has been made, particularly at Reuben Point, where between 300 and 400 residences have been erected.

A 'bus now runs between the town and

Reuben Point, which must prove a great boon to the fortunate residents of that happy locality.

A rather bad sign of the times was reported recently from Lourenço Marques, when the Bishop of the Diocese, during service one Sunday, announced his intention of closing the English Church forthwith unless the parishioners relieved the Church of £16 debt, further adding that he personally was tired of paying the rent of the Church out of his own pocket!

To return again to the harbour works, the following account will show clearly the *modus operandi* of the Portuguese in this respect. "£300,000 was the modest sum required to reclaim some 350 acres of waste ground (mud banks) adjoining the town to the east. At the time it was plainly decreed (provided this sum was forthcoming) it was to be spent in building a river frontage wall of concrete blocks of sufficient length and depth for steamers and ships to lie alongside, discharging cargoes cheaply and expeditiously. The work of filling in or reclaiming the large area of 350 acres to an average depth of 20 feet was to be given out in sections to the contractors. The net results on paper were: First, the sanitary arrangements would be improved by filling in 350 acres of swamp ground, so detrimental to the town and its cosmopolitan inhabitants; second, if £300,000 were spent in harbour works Delagoa Bay would then be well up with its rivals, Natal, East London, and Port Elizabeth; third, the land so reclaimed would realise a million sterling if offered as sites for bonded stores and warehouses in connection with the railway, providing ample room in the future for the extension of the cramped-up town.

"The £300,000 asked for was easily obtained (in Paris, so it is said) for so laudable an undertaking—a mere trifle in comparison with the millions advanced in London to assist Portugal in her financial troubles during the present century.

"The Delagoa Bay harbour works for which this sum of money was advanced twelve months ago (1898) need some explanation. Everything in connection with landing is of the most primitive description. Little or no progress has been made in landing since Delagoa Bay became a port. True, the Portuguese Government have provided cranes in plenty, but there is no deep-water wharf in existence. At half and low tides every loaded lighter is high and dry. The Lisbon Government being in possession of £300,000, no record is published of the probable filtration which this sum was subject to at the hands of the various members of the Government in power. All that was known in Delagoa Bay was so many millions of reis had arrived in Lourenço Marques to be spent on the much required harbour improvements. The residents naturally expected sections of the work would be given out in contracts, and a share of the work divided amongst those who were willing to take the risk of prompt settlements. In this the inhabitants of Lourenço Marques met the first great disappointment. The local Government got hold of the money, and stuck to it, the little real work that has been accomplished having been entirely done by Government officials.

"The first portion of the work entailed the levelling and making of an esplanade at the bottom of the cliff from the town to Reuben Point, a distance of two miles. The military engineers erected a dry stone wall without foundation on the sand shore, ostensibly to protect sections of the sand esplanade. But the periodical high tides and rough weather on a lee shore persistently undid the work of the staff surveyors and engineers employed thereon. The continuous zeal displayed by them was worthy of a better cause. About five hundred concrete blocks, weighing from two to three tons, composed of conglomerated oyster rock, sand and cement, present a formidable appearance as a centrepiece to the harbour works. On close inspection, however, one finds that each block is materially depreciating on exposure to the rigours of this climate. The native labour employed, supervised by soldiers, in manufacturing concrete, has not proved a success, more especially when the concrete blocks are to be submerged in a deep, strong tidal river where no attempt has yet been made to discover the depth of the necessary foundations underneath the mud.

"An experiment was made a few months back in transporting one of the concrete blocks by the aid of a valuable new locomotive crane. A jetty, extending seaward with a sharp decline, was the improvised scene, but the crane took charge of the driver, finally depositing itself headlong into the river. After a fortnight's work this valuable piece of machinery was rescued from its mud-bed, but any further experiments in this particular department have been avoided by the management.

"From three to four hundred natives have been employed from time to time in filling in. About 30 acres out of 350 have been reclaimed. As no provision was made for draining this loose ground, the summer rains descended as is their wont, and washed away many hundreds of tons from the top, whilst the uncontrollable spring tides and waves played sad havoc with the unprotected sand base. The loose drift sand thus washed away is deposited by the outgoing tide at the entrance of the harbour. A bar is slowly but surely accumulating there, which hitherto was unknown.

"To expedite the works a mine was sunk at the top of the cliff, overlooking a portion of the ground to be reclaimed. It was intended to dislodge many thousands of tons of rock and "muck" by blasting. Two thousand pounds of powder, so it is said, was placed in the mine, and an electric wire attached for safety's sake, but the day the explosion should have taken place a deluge of rain fell, half-filling the mine.

"Unfortunately the staff were again to be disappointed by the elements. Eventually, when the explosion did take place, its effect did not tally with the well-thought-out calculations on paper.

"A number of commodious iron houses for the workmen, and extensive offices for the heads of departments have been erected, also huts for natives. Workshops are dotted about, and a large quantity of railway construction material, purchased from the unfortunate Silati Railway, is on the spot, but so far unused. A new tug from Germany, a launch, some lighters, boats

ROAD LEADING FROM DELAGOA BAY.

and boat-houses, complete the assets of this undertaking. Very little work is going on, and the large staff have been subject to an all-round reduction."

To further illustrate the extraordinary and occult methods of the Portuguese colonial officials and the crass ignorance of their employés, I give the following amusing account *in extenso*. " Not many months since, the following episode in commercial life happened at Lourenço Marques. The scene was the wharf, where activity, none too stimulating at the best of times, was really in evidence, some 1,500 natives, men and women, being employed with the assistance of *sjamboks*, in discharging various lighters of cargoes. The time was about nine o'clock in the morning. An order had been issued a short time previous by the Director of Customs prohibiting dynamite from being discharged amongst general merchandise at this spot—an order worthy of strict obedience. About this particular time two French steamship companies entered into competition for Transvaal trade, *viâ* Delagoa Bay. Some encouragement was held out to French mining companies in Johannesburg and exporters in France by the aforesaid French steamship companies in the carriage of special goods at special rates, such packages being marked 'Demi metre.' During the morning of the day alluded to, a Portuguese soldier on duty on the wharf, not having received the benefit of a school board education in the country which gave him birth, imagined in his zealous ignorance that cases marked 'Demi metre' meant dynamite. He having made this important discovery, hastened to the official chamber of the Director of Customs.

"It must be understood a Director of Customs in a Portuguese dependency is appointed by the King of Portugal. There is much dignity and prerogative embodied in his high position, which raise a mortal to a station on a par with the gods in Delagoa Bay. When an act in direct disobedience to edicts and mandates is reported to the Director of Customs in Delagoa Bay, the said act being committed by those foreign menials at work on the wharf and in lighters, duly discovered and reported by one of the King's soldiers, there is certain to be an official mental cyclone in the throne-room of this important department. A fiat was issued instanter by the Director of Customs himself, 'to stop all work on the wharf immediately.' By this time the hour had arrived for official breakfasting. The Director betook himself to his villa away up on the hill. Portuguese breakfasts are naturally late, and consist of many courses and wines. Whether or no the Director of Customs sought consolation in a siesta afterwards there is no evidence to show, but he had not returned to his official duties by three o'clock on that same day.

"More than 1,500 people on the wharf remained idle. Landing agents and local merchants and those employers of labour not understanding this unexpected and unchronicled Portuguese holiday, at length went to the then Governor, who listened attentively and courteously to the complaints. The commercial myrmidons, being assured of His Excellency's sympathy and promises, retired.

"At four o'clock the Director of Customs was 'At Home' in his official chamber in the Customs House. All those in charge of landing goods were ordered to be brought before him. He rated them in round terms for their many delinquencies, especially enumerating the charge of landing dynamite on this particular morning, contrary to his proclamation. The fact of no one owning up to the accusation did not help to lessen the deep-rooted suspicions of the Director. The Portuguese soldier was at length called in, and he pointed out the unfortunate culprit. It certainly looked awkward for the accused, but he, hailing from the Emerald Island, was quite equal to the occasion, and prepared to face the music.

"After some brisk skirmishes in Portuguese and the *taal* of old Ireland, an interpreter was called in, when the soldier's evidence made clear to Patrick 'what all the pother was about twixt him and the light dragoon.' He lodged a protest against being tried, incriminated and sentenced right away; he further suggested the so-called cases of dynamite should be produced. After some more delay the Portuguese soldier appeared with a case marked 'demi metre.' Pat remarked, with a merry twinkle in his eye, that the case should be opened, but suggested with droll humour that more than ordinary care should be used, as the contents might explode.

"The case was opened by the Portuguese searchers in the courtyard. To make a somewhat long story short, the contents of the case marked 'demi metre' were found to be nothing more dangerous than firebricks in transit for Johannesburg.

"Work was again permitted by the Director of Customs to be resumed on the wharf. But fifteen hundred natives had to be paid fifteen hundred half-crowns, all the same, for their enforced idleness by those who employed them.

"The subsequent scene in which the Director of Customs and the Portuguese soldier took the leading rôles will never be known. If some attempt at amends had been made at the time, this strange piece of history, like many such relating to the humours of Delagoa Bay, would have most probably ended in oblivion."

These sort of episodes, and even much worse, could be repeated *ad nauseam*, but sufficient has been said to show the Portuguese style and methods of conducting affairs. Surely it is high time that a nation capable of managing this country and properly administrating its affairs should obtain possession and control, and it now devolves upon the Paramount Power, with its pre-emptive rights, to complete arrangements whereby the cession of the bay and the Portuguese East African territory should be promptly made.

CHAPTER IV

THE NATIVES, FAUNA AND FLORA, ETC.

THE natives of Delagoa Bay and the surrounding country of Gazaland are, as a rule, well set-up and powerful men and women. Their skins are mostly quite black, and they are fairly tall, though the coast natives cannot boast either the same stature or physique as their brethren of the interior. The women are, as a general rule, very much shorter than the men, but they are well proportioned and very powerful, this being accounted for to a large extent, I presume, from the fact that they do nearly all the work.

There are numerous tribes, mostly small ones, under the control of petty chiefs, who owe allegiance to the Portuguese. The largest of the tribes are to be found in the neighbourhood of the Manissa river, and are known respectively as Mupunga's tribe and Sishassi's tribe. Large tribes are also to be found at Matolla and Catembe, while the Poulana, Mahota, and Mashequene natives belong to only very small tribes. Looking at the number of different tribes, it is not to be wondered at that some of them should occasionally rebel, and also that tribal fights should occur when it is remembered that the Portuguese were powerless to control them formerly, and even now they are not completely under subjection. Some of the tribes are so small that they are hardly worthy of the name, and have only insignificant "kraals," under petty chiefs, who are of no account whatsoever outside their own particular tribe. By constant intermarriage they have now become very mixed, and many of them have a strain of Portuguese blood in their veins.

The Zulu Napoleon, the great chief T'Chaka, played havoc with the Portuguese who had established various miserable little stations at different points in Gazaland, and not only destroyed their settlements and routed their forces, but seriously reduced the various native tribes. The Abagaza also ravaged the country around and spread desolation far and wide. One of T'Chaka's generals, a man named Manikoos, was sent by that mighty warrior to take possession of Delagoa Bay. This, however, he was unable to effect, so he turned his attention to the northern districts, and was so successful that he conquered the whole of the country lying between the Limpopo and the Zambesi.

The coast natives can hardly be said to have greatly benefited by the civilising process, as civilisation is taught by the Portuguese. The Portuguese have always experienced the greatest difficulty in governing the various tribes which are nominally under their control. From Delagoa Bay to the Zambesi river there are numerous tribes who have persistently in the past defied the Portuguese authority, and oftentimes successfully. It is only quite recently that order has been restored and some sort of control established over the natives. In 1892 war was declared against the chief Makombi, who was ultimately defeated, and later serious trouble was caused by the paramount chief of Gazaland, Gungunhana, which necessitated another war. Portugal was again victorious, and succeeded not only in defeating his army, but also in capturing the chief. Since this time the natives have been fairly quiet, and have caused little serious disturbance.

The natives of Gazaland are extremely independent, and have a rooted objection to work of any description. This is chiefly to be accounted for by the fact that the country is so rich, having a most fertile soil, that they can live comfortably and supply all their wants with very little labour required. They formerly paid, in a slipshod kind of way, a tribute of mealies, &c., to the Government, which was never rigidly enforced, but now a hut tax is levied, and is regularly collected.

The untutored natives in many respects resemble the monkey tribe very closely. They are extremely imitative, but are unfortunately more apt in acquiring the white man's vices than in emulating his virtues. Inland, where there are many petty tribes under small chiefs, who have not come into contact with the Portuguese to the same extent, the natives are fine manly fellows, with simple tastes, and a fairish code of morals. Of course one must not expect too high a standard of morals from people who are practically savages, but at the same time they can put to the blush (if that be possible) some of the neighbouring tribes who have taken a lesson from their Portuguese masters in civilisation.

The principal curse of the natives, both men and women, is drink. They give way to it on any and every possible occasion, and a Kafir in drink is a dangerous beast. They consume their native beer, *chuala*, in tremendous quantities, and that is of course bad enough; but it is quite innocuous as compared with the fiery spirits introduced by the European. Rum is the drink *par excellence*, and a horrible decoction it is, practically converting them into temporary lunatics. The women are nearly, if not quite, as bad as the men. The Kafirs are confirmed snuff-takers, and every Kafir boasts his snuff-box, usually a small gourd, as a rule ornamented with brass wire, to which they have constant recourse. Through a large hole in the lobe of the ear is often carried a snuff-spoon, which is in many cases a beautifully carved piece of bone. The Kafirs are extremely clever at carving, and do their work both neatly and artistically. The snuff is taken from the gourd or other box into the spoon and a liberal dose of it snuffed up with the keenest relish. Curiously enough, it is the " fair sex "—if this term can be applied to the native women—who do most of the smoking, they leaving the snuff-taking principally to their lords and masters. The women smoke a good deal, and even quite young women enjoy sucking at the short pipe. Kafirs to a large extent smoke *m'bangi*, which is made from the wild hemp and is a strong soporific. The native language is " Landi," and is common to many tribes.

The dress of the Kafirs in the interior is principally noted for its extreme simplicity.

THE NATIVES, FAUNA AND FLORA, ETC.

The *moutje*, an arrangement of bits of hide or tails, tied to a piece of string and hung round the waist, is the chief article of dress; the rest of the toilet being made up of brass bangles and bead ornaments. In town, however, they wear shirts and sometimes trousers, or, if not, a *capalane*, which is a gaudy-coloured handkerchief tied round the waist. The women also wear these *capalanes*, only they reach somewhat lower, and have in addition a coloured cloth which goes round the chest. They wear an enormous quantity of brass and iron wire bangles both around the arms and the ankles, the weight of these combined ornaments being extremely great, although they appear to cause their wearers no inconvenience whatever. When the curious native dance is being indulged in, which consists for the most part of violently stamping on the ground with both feet, which produces a dull thud, these bangles assist the performance to a certain extent by the jangle they cause, and this is completed by the curious chant of the dancers. The singing cannot be described as particularly melodious, for all their songs have the same monotonous sounds repeated *ad nauseam*. True, they have a very good effect when there are numbers combining in the dance, only one does not want too prolonged an entertainment. The Kafirs invariably sing at their work, and this seems of great assistance to them; when not singing they are whistling, which latter accomplishment they are about as proficient in as the former. However, it makes them happy, and really seems to aid them in their work. They have two or three different kinds of musical instruments, which produce excruciating noises much appreciated by the natives. The music is doubtless of a highly classical order, there being a distinct absence of "tune."

The natives estimate their wealth by the number of wives and cattle they possess. The wives themselves are purchased either with cattle or with money. Since the rinderpest scourge cattle have become so scarce that money has to suffice. The value of a woman depends very much upon her build, her stoutness of limbs, and general

THE NATIVES, FAUNA AND FLORA, ETC.

capability for work; the price running from £4 or £5 to about £20, which latter sum is considered a good figure. Should the woman turn out to be unsatisfactory the wonderful custom prevails that not only can she be sent back to her own people, but that they will refund her husband the price paid for her.

The natives wear blue when in mourning. For two or three days after a death has taken place the relatives and friends alternate their crying with eating and drinking galore—in fact, a regular Irish wake. All the belongings of the deceased are buried with him, and the hut he occupied is forsaken, and remains thus until it crumbles away.

Tattooing is not much practised by the natives, although occasionally some of the women tattoo their faces. The women also have a curious custom of smearing their bodies with red ochre some time before and after child-birth.

Kafirs have an odour which is peculiar to them and is not appreciated by the white man. When a kraal is in the vicinity there is no mistaking the fact, for a conglomeration of smells making a most disagreeable compound of pungent character immediately assails the nostrils.

The natives are without doubt a latent source of wealth to the country, and when a good example is set them, and they can be induced to assist in the thorough cultivation of the land, as well as in the mines, another splendid and permanent industry will be fostered, and one that will endure and prove an immense source of revenue to the country long after the lives of the gold mines have been spent.

Amongst the animals to be found in the country surrounding Delagoa Bay and stretching inland to the Lebombo Mountains, pride of place must of course be given to the lion, although lions are now much more scarce than formerly, as are also hyenas, tigers, and leopards. A fair trade used to be carried on in their skins, but this has almost entirely fallen off.

A curious incident recently occurred on the line near Komati Poort. A large tiger was in the act of crossing the line as a train was approaching. The cow-catcher on the engine just caught it and nearly cut it in two, and yet when the driver got down to haul the body off the line the brute snapped at him.

Antelopes are fairly numerous and consist of many varieties—blesbok, springbok, hartebeests, the blue wildebeest, gemsbok—with splendid antlers running as a rule about thirty-seven to forty inches in length; rietbuck, with peculiar circular marks on the hind-quarters; bushbuck, with spiral horns; and, in the neighbourhood of the Lebombos, large herds of *M'Pala* (red-buck). The country near the Lebombo Mountains swarms with herds of antelope and buck of every description. Here can be seen occasionally a small herd of quagga—graceful creatures with yellow skins and black stripes.

Among the smaller kinds of antelope is to be found the pretty and graceful little klipspringer, which is wonderfully surefooted, and jumps from rock to rock like a chamois. They are usually to be seen in seemingly the most dangerous positions on mountain heights.

The springbok and wildebeest before mentioned are both marvellous jumpers; these jumps not necessarily being taken to get over some obstacle, but out of sheer exuberance of spirits, their antics being wonderful to behold. There are also the pretty little duiker and steinbok, both of which are excellent eating and make splendid biltong.

Buffalo are now very scarce, and unless some strict means of preservation are provided will inevitably become extinct. Mr. Rhodes is doing much to preserve the various species of South African animals, and has set a very good and praiseworthy example by establishing a most extensive and magnificent collection in the beautiful grounds of his Cape Town residence, Groote Schuur. What is really wanted, however, is an extremely large area of land, properly enclosed, say in Central Africa, where there is any amount of suitable land to spare, and where the various species that are fast becoming rare may have an opportunity of breeding and multiplying undisturbed by hunters, prospectors, and sportsmen.

Further, a close season should be rigidly enforced, and game licenses required. Something is being done in this direction, but it needs properly carrying out at an early date to be effectual.

Birds of various kinds are to be met with around Delagoa Bay, from the big *paauw*, or bustard, to the little finches and other small birds.

Knorhaan, which are excellent eating, are pretty plentiful in parts. *Partridges, guinea-fowl, quail, plover* and other game birds are found. Small birds exist in large quantities, and although not noted for their singing propensities usually make up for it by the brightness and even gaudiness of their plumage. The *sun-birds* have pretty metallic coloured feathers and many of the *finches* have very gay colours. *Bigodas*, which are pretty little birds, sing charmingly. *Starlings, woodpeckers, waxbills*— extremely handsome birds with blue colours —*kingfishers, owls* of different species, *pigeons, doves, weaver-birds* (which make the curious pendent nests), *swallows, wagtails, goat-suckers* (which make a horrible screeching sound), *whydah-finches* (with peculiar long, narrow tails), and many other varieties of small birds abound.

Then there are the birds of prey—*hawks* and *falcons* and the *aasvogel*, or vulture, which is a splendid scavenger.

Snakes are very numerous in the wooded districts. Some of them have very pretty markings, but many are poisonous and to be avoided if possible. Occasionally the large *cobra* is seen, also the curious *puff-adder*, while *mambas*, both of the brown and green varieties, are very plentiful.

Rats and mice, moles, *zorillas*, *simbas*, or wild cats, hares, and many other small animals are to be found everywhere. Lizards, iguanas, of very pretty colours, and chameleons are common. As for insects, their name is legion. There are spiders of all kinds, some being huge, horrible things; flies of many varieties—some pretty, but all troublesome—insects with curious bodies like bits of stick, mosquitoes, scorpions, centipedes, grasshoppers, locusts, the *Hottentot god*, or "praying-mantis," red and white ants, both sorts being most destructive, and large black ants which smell abominably if touched; beetles of infinite varieties, cockroaches, peculiar little bugs, the ubiquitous and tantalising flea, horrible little lice, and a host of other creatures and insects of all kinds abound and flourish exceedingly. Butterflies and moths are very numerous, and many kinds are both wonderful and beautiful, as are the different species of dragonflies to be found in this country.

The shores around Delagoa Bay are mostly swampy and therefore suited to the growth of the *mangrove*, which flourishes in all directions. These mangroves form a perfect fringe to the shores and prevent them from appearing as bare and inhospitable as they otherwise would do.

Inland the soil is rich although sandy in parts, and is covered in all directions with small patches of bush, principally the various kinds of *acacia*, the common mimosa thorn. One species of acacia (*Cæsalpinia bonducella*) grows to a good height, and is thickly covered with thorns all over, as is the *Acacia horrida*, which is commonly found in the neighbourhood of watercourses.

There are numerous kinds of indiarubber-trees and many varieties of flowering trees and bushes, some of which bear very lovely flowers, particularly one specimen (*Tecoma capensis*), a fine bush with a gaudy scarlet flower, which is peculiar inasmuch as it flowers three times a year.

Some of the creepers are very curious and bear many flowers, more or less pretty and fanciful.

The *Euphorbiæ*, or *spurge-plants*, have much the appearance of cacti, although the flower is quite different. They can, however, be easily identified by slightly puncturing the skin, when a viscous milky juice will flow from the incision. The sap is an admirable substitute for indiarubber, and makes excellent waterproofing. One species of euphorbia, having very thin branches, has an interesting appearance and grows freely. The accompanying illustration will serve to give an idea of its curious thin spiky branches. It is often planted over graves by the Kafirs.

THIN-BRANCHED EUPHORBIA.
Sketched by the Author.

THE NATIVES, FAUNA AND FLORA, ETC.

Field flowers grow plentifully, and some varieties are extremely pretty, with very fanciful shades of colours. The Kafirs have some skill as herbalists, and make use of many plants and herbs as medicines.

Very pretty are the different coloured species of *Hibiscus*, some being upright and others of the trailing variety.

A very curious plant to be found at Delagoa Bay is the *Bryophyllum*, for if the leaves be placed on moist ground they will sprout at each of the notches and actually grow fresh plants from the leaves. Then there are many different kinds of orchids, aloes, and pretty creepers.

Pumpkins are very numerous, as are also water-melons and pineapples. Orange-trees are found in parts as well as mango and guava-trees, although they do not grow very abundantly. The lemon-tree is occasionally found, but the most common is the banana, which grows nearly everywhere. The Kafir orange, which may be described as being "bitter-sweet," grows in different parts, but the best kinds are to be found in the

Catembe and Matolla districts, where the fruit attains to a large size.

There are many varieties of the wild fig (from which a decoction is brewed) and bush fig, the *Anana*, the *Baobab*, and others, as well as many species of *gourds*, some of which are edible and pleasant eating, while others are extremely bitter. These gourds are of all sizes, and the Kafirs utilise them for a variety of purposes. The small ones they ornament with brass and copper wire and use as snuff-boxes, and the larger ones serve as water and beer-jugs, &c.

The *Grenadilla* and the *Shaddock* are to be found; the latter being pulpy and juicy, is beautifully cool and refreshing in the hot weather.

The *egg-plant* bears an excellent fruit, called "Berenjelas," which, properly cooked, is very succulent.

The indiarubber plant grows in all directions, and when the country is properly opened up this useful industry should flourish exceedingly and prove very lucrative.

Palm-trees are numerous and are extremely useful. In the neighbourhood of Poulana, beyond Mashequene, they are very plentiful. The natives make deep incisions in the trees and hang up gourds to catch the palm wine, which is very sweet to the taste until fermentation begins. The leaves of the palm make excellent baskets, and the natives are very expert at manufacturing them.

Tree-ferns are common, as are the various kinds of thorn and prickly plants—some of which grow in large thickets and are absolutely impassable, such as the *Doornboom*. The *wait-a-bit* thorn, or, as the Dutch call it, *Wagt een beetje*, is an aggravating one, and its name fully explains why.

Amongst the different kinds of vegetables to be found may be mentioned beans, sweet potatoes, cabbages, mealies, mandioca root, &c. ; but all kinds of vegetables are very scarce, and very little trouble or attention appears to be given to the growth of them. The soil is so rich that with a little energy and care in the cultivation, together with proper irrigation, anything could be made to grow easily and abundantly. The natives grow very little more than what suffices for their own use, and the Portuguese are too dilatory to trouble themselves about the matter.

Ground-nuts are very plentiful and easy to grow, and when nicely cooked are excellent eating. They produce a valuable oil and deserve cultivation, as the exportation of the oil should prove lucrative, as should that of the *castor-oil* plant.

Besides mealies—which may be described as being the staple article of diet of the natives—millet and *mabele*, or Kafir-corn, are very largely grown. From these latter, *chuala*, a kind of beer, is made, and is drunk to an enormous extent by the natives; the manufacture of it being the exclusive province of the women.

Rice is cultivated in some districts, principally about Makota and Poulana, but it is not extensively grown, although it would pay exceedingly well to do so. Rice requires a fair amount of moisture, consequently until the land is properly irrigated it cannot be grown on a very large scale, sufficient for exportation.

There are different kinds of grasses, some having a rather pretty appearance, although the pleasing varieties are, generally speaking, not so good for pasture.

CHAPTER V

THE DELAGOA BAY AND NETHERLANDS RAILWAYS

THE history of the Delagoa Bay Railway is certainly a curious one. It has had its vicissitudes. From very early days the Boers saw the policy of trying to establish a means of communication with the coast, and as Delagoa Bay is the natural port of the Transvaal, they have ever schemed to obtain an interest there. It is obvious that a line of railway to the coast is of the first importance to the Transvaal, and for many years past the powers at Pretoria have sought to construct a railway to some coast port. The Boers want, and always have wanted, an outlet; without it they are practically crippled.

Long ago the King of Portugal granted

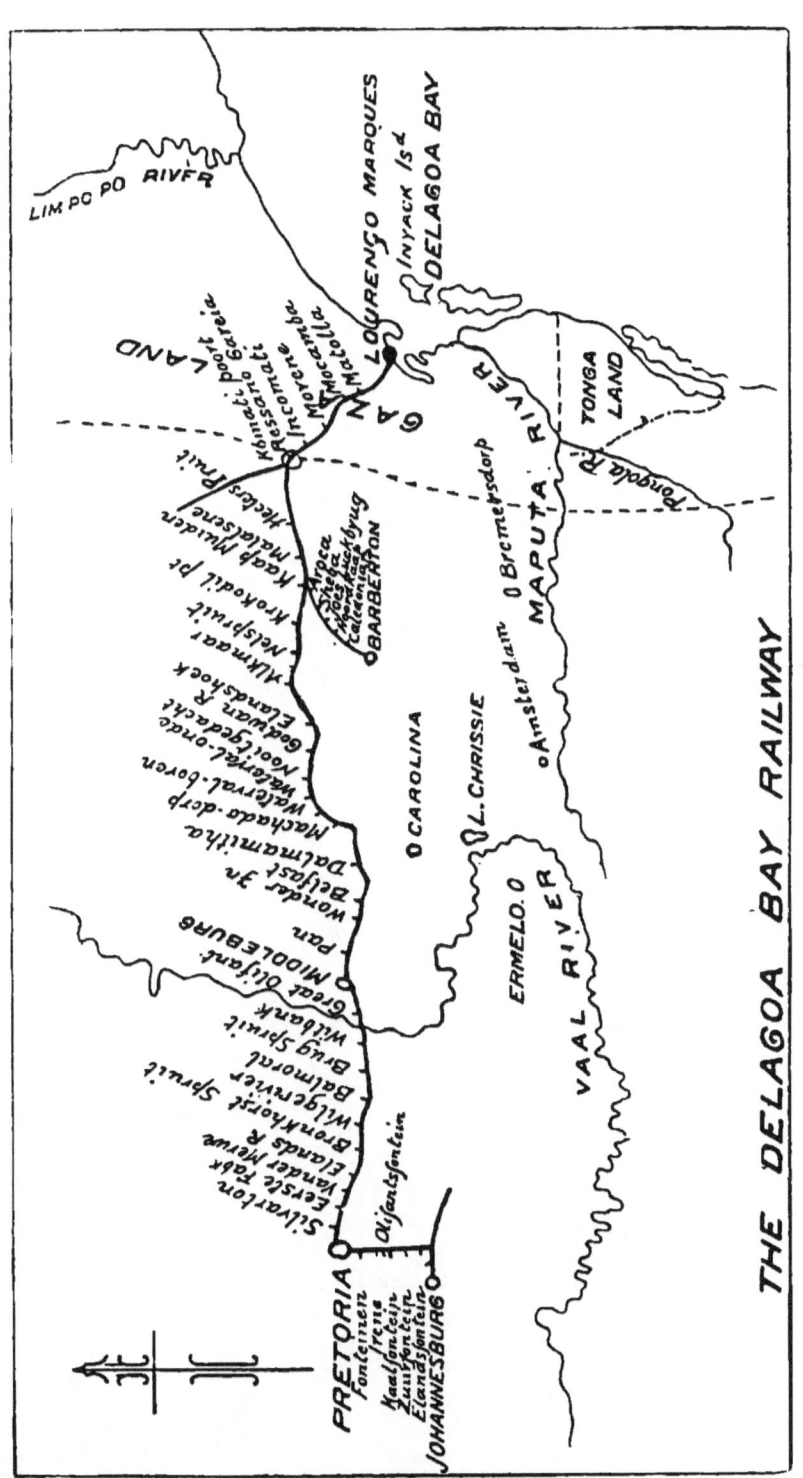

SKETCH MAP BY THE AUTHOR.

concessions for the construction of a railway from the Bay to Pretoria, but nothing ever came of them. One of these concessions was granted to a Mr. Moodie, but after a considerable lapse of time the undertaking fell through. Again, however, in January, 1873, Mr. Moodie got another concession for the railway, but as he was not able to obtain the capital required to carry through the work within the specified time, Mr. Burgers (who was then the President of the Transvaal) determined that the Government should take up the work itself. The Government, however, was badly in need of funds, so the President came over to Europe to raise a loan, but in this he was not very successful. He could do no good in England, so went to Holland, where he obtained nearly £80,000 on the strength of a commercial treaty obtained from Portugal. He then arranged with a Belgian firm for a supply of rails for the railway, amounting to about £64,000. Only half of these rails were consigned to Delagoa Bay, the other half being stored in the different Belgian and Holland ports ; until in 1879 they were taken over by the British Government.

In 1876 Portugal granted a further concession to Moodie, giving him the right to construct that portion of the railway running from Lourenço Marques to the Lebombo. Mr. Moodie was again unsuccessful, and the Transvaal Republic gave him £5,000 to surrender his concession. This concession was subsequently transferred by the Transvaal Government to a company, formed in Pretoria, called the "Lebombo Railway Company, Limited," having a nominal capital of £110,000, two-thirds of which were subscribed by the Government, and part of the remainder privately. The company got heavily in debt and soon came to grief, and so it was decided to mortgage or sell some of the stock and plant stored at the Bay. While negotiations were pending with the Portuguese Government with a view to the possible sale of the plant, Great Britain appeared on the scene and took possession of the country, and the Lebombo Railway Company was dissolved.

The British Government ordered a new survey of the line in May, 1879, but nothing was done.

Towards the end of 1883 the Portuguese Government granted a new concession for the construction of a line from Delagoa Bay to Komati Poort, but no developments took place until March, 1887, when Colonel Edward McMurdo, who was a citizen of the United States, formed a company in London, having a share capital of £500,000, to construct the line under this concession. About the middle of the year the works were put in hand and pushed forward so actively that the railway was completely finished by November in the following year.

On the 1st of November the completion of the line was announced by the Portuguese Government, but on the following day an intimation reached London from Sir Thomas Tancred, the contractor, that they were waiting for the arrival of the carriages, and consequently the opening would be deferred for a week or two. A despatch dated Durban, December 14th, announced that the first section to Komati was opened on that day by the Governor-General amid great rejoicings.

The distance by the rail from Lourenço Marques to Komati Poort is about fifty-two miles, and traverses a splendid grazing country, which is also highly mineralised. This portion of the line was comparatively easy to lay as it is fairly level, although there are some rather steep gradients in parts.

From the commencement the success of the line was hampered through the action of the Transvaal Government in imposing excessive tariffs. The Transvaal Government was acting on behalf of the Netherlands Concessionaires, who, under the name of the Netherlands South African Company, had obtained the concessions granted to various persons in Holland, in May, 1885. This company had to continue and complete the line from the terminus at Komati Poort to Pretoria.

As there was a very strong feeling of jealousy and dislike towards the English Company, the Transvaal Government lost no opportunity of trying to wreck it. The Portuguese Government followed suit and found a pretext for raising difficulties by claiming that the line had not been built in accordance with the terms of the concession in that it did not reach the proposed terminus, which was about fifteen miles beyond the then terminus on the banks of the Komati river, which pierces the mountain chain a little to the south of the Northern road to Lydenburg. The Portuguese Government then took steps by demanding that the line be completed within a specified time, or in default that the concession should be forfeited, together with all the plant, rolling stock, and property belonging to the company.

Notwithstanding the fact that the company vigorously resisted the contention of the Government, Portugal in June, 1889, arbitrarily took possession of the railway and the whole of its property.

The company naturally wished to submit a case to arbitration, but this the Portuguese Government would not allow, until it was forced to do so by reason of the intervention of Great Britain and the United States.

At this time the controlling interest in the share capital of the company was owned by the widow of the concessionaire, Colonel McMurdo, who had then recently died.

The following particulars I take from an account relating to the subsequent dealings in the matter: "On the seizure of the railway by the Portuguese Government, the rights of Mrs. McMurdo were vigorously asserted by Mr. Blain, the then Secretary of State at Washington, who insisted on a prompt reparation by Portugal. Lord Salisbury, on behalf of the debenture-holders and shareholders who were British subjects, made a similar demand, and in the autumn of 1890 it was arranged between the three Governments that the amount of compensation payable to the claimants should be determined by three Swiss jurists, to be named by the Swiss President.

"The claims of the parties were afterwards formulated before the Court of Arbitration, the British and American claims being based upon the present and prospective shares and debentures; while an excess in the value claimed on the American side over the shares represented by the British Government was explained by the fact that the McMurdo shares constituted the "control" of the company, and as such had a special value. In justification of this contention documentary evidence was supplied that a syndicate of German bankers had actually offered Colonel McMurdo £700,000 for 25,100 shares of the nominal value of £251,000, which offer he had refused; and that the late Mr. van Blokland, the Transvaal Minister at the Hague, had, in conjunction with the bankers of the Transvaal Government, advised President Kruger to buy the same number of shares for £1,100,000. It was contended by both claimants that, irrespective of any market price for the shares, the intrinsic value of the concession was such that the shares were worth even more than the sum claimed for them, and in proof of this the reports of several engineers were furnished which attributed to the concession a value of £3,000,000 and upwards. In reply to these claims the Portuguese Government contended that it had legal justification in seizing the railway, and that a proper compensation to the claimants would be the mere repayment of the sums which had actually been expended in the construction of the railway.

"The pleadings were finally closed in the summer of 1896, and the Arbitration Court then announced its intention to appoint a technical commission to advise it as to the value of the railway construction, and also of the concession, according to the varying theories of the contending parties. The choice fell upon M. Stockalper, M. Dietler, and M. Nicole, three Swiss engineers of indisputable eminence, the commission being finally constituted with the concurrence of all parties.

"In December, 1896, M. Nicole left for South Africa to make a local inspection, returning to Europe in April, 1897. The report of this commission was long delayed, and it was not until the month of March,

1898, that it was filed, when ample excuse for the delay was found in the comprehensive and exhaustive manner in which the experts had fulfilled their task.

"The result of the inquiry made by the experts may shortly be summarised as follows, but it must be borne in mind that their conclusions were in no way binding on the Court, and constituted nothing in the nature of a judgment, though of course they would naturally carry weight as being the opinion of assessors especially appointed by the Court.

"In reply to a question propounded by the Portuguese Government, based upon its contention that the claimants were only entitled to the value of the railway construction, the experts replied that the value of the construction at the time of its seizure was £255,000.

"In reply to a second question by the same Government as to what was the value of the concession at the date of the seizure, in view of the fact that the last section of the line had not been built, and that it was exceedingly doubtful whether the Transvaal connection would ever be built, the experts stated that the commercial value of the concession at that date was £1,100,000.

"In reply to a question put by the claiming Governments as to what was the value of the concession at the time of the local inspection made by M. Nicole, the experts said that on the 31st December, 1896, its value was £1,800,000.

"These results were arrived at by assuming an annual increase in the traffic over the railway of 10 per cent., with working expenses at 56 per cent., and allowing to the Delagoa line 25 per cent. only of the traffic, as against 43 per cent. which they allowed for the Cape line, and 32 per cent. which they conceded to the Natal line.

"The report gave some interesting particulars as to the remarkable advance which had taken place as to the value of land at Lourenço Marques within the past few years. Thus land in the town which was worth but a shilling or two in 1889 now sells for £22 per square metre. So a house in the town which a few years since was sold for £600 had recently been sold for £10,000. The advance in prices had been equally marked in lands outside the town, which had become valuable for private residences.

"Having given the parties a reasonable time for the consideration of the report, the Court, on the 9th May, 1898, requested them within a month to file any observations they wished to make on the report, and to set out any further questions that they wished to put to the experts.

"The parties availed themselves freely of this invitation. The Portuguese Government then submitted the report to a fourth expert in the person of Dr. Escher, an eminent Swiss engineer. Under his guidance they vigorously criticised the report as assigning an undue value to the concession. The British and American Governments, while accepting the report in the main and freely acknowledging the ability and fairness which characterised it, took exception to it on two or three points, in which they thought the experts had not gone far enough. They were of opinion that the legitimate share of the Delagoa Bay line in the Transvaal traffic should be at least one-third, instead of one-quarter, as assigned to it. They pointed out that by an oversight the experts had omitted to value about 6,000 acres of land in the neighbourhood of Lourenço Marques, belonging to the company, which, on the basis of the value assigned to such land by experts, would be worth at least £1,000,000, and would add that amount to the value of the concession.

"In order to hasten the conclusion of the arbitration the three Governments agreed to forego the oral argument with which it was intended to close the proceedings, and to substitute for it a succinct *resumé* of the facts and arguments adduced by them."

These arbitration proceedings have deservedly been termed the "modern Jarndyce *v.* Jarndyce case." The dispute was first referred to arbitration towards the end of the year 1890, and since then the case has dragged on its weary length year after year, without the end seemingly being any nearer in view. True, the work to be done has been great, but the time occupied is out of all proportion, and the members of the original syndicate must long since have experienced that sickness which hope deferred is popularly reported to have upon the heart.

However, the arbitrators' award cannot be delayed for ever, and we must surely now be within a measurable distance of obtaining it. The experts' report has been laid before the Court, and this must of necessity form a very strong guide to the arbitrators' decision, and it is extremely difficult to conceive how it is possible for any lengthened delay now to occur. Consequently we may expect to receive the award during this present year of grace.

Some time ago the Portuguese Government paid over a sum of £28,000 on account of their obligations to the shareholders of the company.

In the month of June, 1895, the whole

of the line from Delagoa Bay to Pretoria was formally opened, and as the railway from the Cape to the Transvaal had been completed in September, 1892, Johannesburg was placed in direct communication with Delagoa Bay *viâ* Pretoria. This railway has opened up a number of fine goldfields, such as the Komati, Lydenburg, and De Kaap goldfields. Soon, no doubt, a branch line, probably an extension of the line from Barberton, will run through that extremely rich but little developed country of Swaziland.

The Delagoa Bay Railway, which is a very good bit of engineering, is under 400 miles long—that is, from Lourenço Marques to Johannesburg—and the journey occupies less than twenty-four hours. The scenery on some parts of the line is really very charming and picturesque. Delagoa Bay is about 348 miles by rail from Pretoria, 55 miles from Komati, 67 miles from Barberton—which is in the heart of the De Kaap goldfields—and some 200 miles from the Lydenburg goldfields.

Some portion of the country over which

the line is laid is of a very difficult and dangerous character, and many lives were lost in the construction of the line. Leaving the railway station at Lourenço Marques, the line runs over a flat bit of country, rather swampy at the start, for a distance of over fifty miles until Komati is reached. From the commencement of the journey the long range of the blue Lebombo Mountains looms large on the horizon.

All this portion of the country is extremely fertile, the vegetation being of the most luxurious tropical character. If this land was placed under cultivation, almost anything could be grown, particularly mealies, sugar, tobacco, &c.

The line follows the direction of the Komati river, which is a very fine and picturesque one. The line leads across the river, not far from the point where the Komati joins the Crocodile, and then follows the latter river. Between this point and Komati Poort is a wide valley that has an unenviable notoriety as being a hotbed of malarial fever, and is a most desolate district. Ressano Garcia is the small frontier town on the border of Gazaland, and after passing this station Komati Poort is quickly reached and Transvaal territory gained. The character of the country on this side of the Lebombos is totally different, being wild and rugged, and a higher altitude is reached. The train follows a very tortuous route; now it curves round some precipitous mountain-side, the depth to the valley below being quite awe-inspiring, as in the case of the Elands Valley, and anon it descends such steep declivities that one trembles to think what would happen if the brakes failed. This rugged character of the country is maintained until the famous range of mountains known as the Drakensberg is reached. The line is ever mounting upwards, laboriously ascending steep gradients, until it comes at a great altitude to the "high veld" of the Transvaal. A most perfect panorama is presented to the eyes of the astonished and delighted traveller. The difference in the temperature is very marked, for this plateau is over 6,000 feet above the level of the sea. To accomplish this tremendous climb the

A STATION ON THE DELAGOA BAY RAILWAY.
Reproduced by permission from "South Africa."

line is laid on the cog-wheel system, a specially constructed engine having of course to be attached.

The scenery is charming and the view magnificent, while the vegetation grows in wild profusion. The heart of a botanist would be gladdened as he surveyed the magnificent flora and studied the great variety and brilliant colourings of the different species brought before his enraptured gaze.

The line through the Transvaal to Pretoria is known as the " Netherlands " Railway. The carriages are very good and run fairly smoothly, especially looking at the diversified character of the country, and taking into consideration some of the very steep gradients on the line. The line itself is very well laid and carefully ballasted, and is the ordinary South African gauge.

The traffic over the line is continually increasing. During the month of September, 1898, one hundred and eleven trains were made up for the Transvaal, carrying 12,589 tons. During the same month in the preceding year the railway only made up seventy-five trains and carried 10,716 tons, there being a difference in favour of 1898 of 1,873 tons.

CHAPTER VI

THE TRADE, ETC., OF DELAGOA BAY

THE trade of Lourenço Marques has progressed very slowly. In early days it was, of course, confined to mere trafficking with the natives, but gradually, as the settlement at Lourenço Marques grew into a town, and a small permanent population flourished there, a regular trade was established, although necessarily on a very small scale. Until the advent of the railway to Pretoria and Johannesburg, Lourenço Marques remained in a very sleepy and backward state. A certain amount of building had been done, and a small trade was carried on in a desultory manner with the interior, but owing to the difficulties of transport it was, of course, very limited, and this fact prevented all but a very few vessels touching at the port. The trade with the natives chiefly consisted of ivory; but as the population of Lourenço Marques slowly increased their wants had to be supplied, and the increased imports meant a larger amount of shipping, which opened up the port and brought the natural advantages of the harbour more prominently forward.

Notwithstanding the excellence of the harbour, the shipping would have made but little headway, and the town of Lourenço Marques have remained a "sleepy hollow," had it not been for the railway. Again, the railway itself would not have been built but for the opening up of the Transvaal. When the famous goldfields of the Rand were discovered all men's eyes were turned to that wonderful locality, and the immense importance of railway communication between the mushroom town of Johannesburg and Delagoa Bay was immediately felt.

The town of Johannesburg has a truly remarkable record; but a few years ago its present site was nothing but bare veld of an uninteresting character, the monotony of which was only varied by a few corrugated iron shanties. The town progressed by leaps and bounds, and to-day it boasts magnificent public buildings, broad thoroughfares, and all the luxuries and conveniences that a high state of civilisation and a wealthy community alone can bestow.

Of course a line had to be constructed to Delagoa Bay, which by its geographical position is the natural port of the Transvaal. With the opening of the first section of the line from Delagoa Bay to Komati Poort a certain impetus was given to the trade of Lourenço Marques, and when the line was fully completed to Pretoria and Johannesburg the town of Lourenço Marques gradually extended, and the trade and shipping increased.

Had Delagoa Bay been a British possession its prosperity would have been immediately assured. Lourenço Marques would have been metamorphosed into a large, healthy, and flourishing town; the harbour would have been improved by the erection of piers, landing-stages, &c., while the surrounding country would have been opened up. Instead of this, however, the progress made has been of a very slow order under the hands of the procrastinating Portuguese. They seem to adopt precisely the same motto as the Turks, who murmur in a self-satisfied manner, "By and by, plenty time." Still, even the Portuguese were obliged to take cognisance of the fact that they had a glorious possession, and one which would repay a hundredfold any outlay in improvements. Consequently certain works were inaugurated, much was proposed, but comparatively little was done.

The corrupt nature of the Portuguese colonial officials has passed into a byword, and Lourenço Marques has suffered immeasurably from this defect. Excellent works have been prevented or seriously hampered and delayed, trade has been greatly interfered with, and necessary reforms either shelved or only carried out in an unsatisfactory and incomplete manner. Notwithstanding these most potent drawbacks to prosperity and increased financial success, Delagoa Bay flourished entirely owing to its natural advantages.

As the trade slowly improved, and the harbour opened up, so a better class of people were gradually attracted to the place, and shops and stores were built, as well as fine houses in the wisely chosen residential quarter of the town on the fine commanding site known as Reuben Point. All this meant increased shipping and larger imports; still the advance was not, and never has been, commensurate with the extreme ripeness and requirements of the port.

For vessels coming through the Suez Canal and the Red Sea, Delagoa Bay is the natural port of call. Here a vessel can coal and water without any nervous apprehension as to whether she can cross the bar, and she can anchor in the inner harbour close up to the town. The navigable channels are wide and deep, so that there always has been every inducement to encourage shipping by necessary reforms and increased accommodation. Much has been done in the past, but very much remains to be done, and in the immediate future innumerable wise reforms will have to be carried out.

The trade of Lourenço Marques—as a reference to the consular reports for some years past will show—has steadily increased, but is nothing like in proportion to what it should be had a liberal government made the necessary improvements and so given an impetus to trade. Most of the large houses in the town are forwarding houses, and these do very well. Unfortunately, at the present time the bulk of the trade is in the hands of the Orientals. Chinese, Hindoos, and Arabs flourish exceedingly, and this at the expense of the Europeans. We may confidently expect our fellow-countrymen to hold the principal trade of Lourenço Marques, if the port is leased or ceded to Great Britain; and once we are in possession the trade will increase enormously and be well worth the holding.

One great source of income is the navigation coal trade. This trade is, however, seriously hampered, owing to the excessive railway rates imposed on coal drawn from the Middleburg districts.

A Johannesburg authority says: "It is impossible for Transvaal coal, under present excessive railway rates, to compete for the Indian and Australian coaling trade. Under keen freight competition sea-borne coal is sold at Mauritius cheaper than Transvaal coal can be delivered on board at Delagoa. With a reasonable railway tariff Lourenço Marques might within a few years be made the principal coaling station of the Indian Ocean, and a great channel of trade opened to the Transvaal." There is no doubt that in the future Delagoa Bay will become a great coaling station, and this fact alone would be sufficient to ensure the prosperity of the port.

Apart from the coalfields of the Transvaal, however, there are immense coalfields in the fine tract of country lying between Delagoa Bay and the Lebombo Mountains. In this splendid district, which only requires properly opening up, there are extensive coal seams, and experts have pronounced the coal to be of a good quality. Owing to their proximity to Delagoa Bay, and the railway communicating therewith, the mines could be worked economically, and the coal delivered on board at Delagoa Bay at a very reasonable rate. This would give a very great impetus to the trade of the port, and would undoubtedly prove a great financial success to the mines themselves. If necessary, a separate line or branch lines to the fields could be constructed, and this might be made a very paying undertaking, as this portion of the country must be opened up ere long. The land is stated to be rich in minerals, and some very encouraging reports anent this have been received of late.

Accounts are continually coming to hand of fresh discoveries of coal near Delagoa Bay and all over the surrounding country; so that the fields must be of enormous extent. Should we obtain possession, we shall find Delagoa Bay emulating Durban, and making a large contribution of coal for the supply of the British fleet.

Recently rich coal discoveries have been made at Inyack Island, which is situated at the entrance to the Bay. It is stated that the discovery will be invaluable for shipping, and is expected to revolutionise the trade of the East Coast of Africa. Baron d'Inhaca, who is the titular lord of the island and the owner of nearly all the rights therein, recently started extensive boring operations, and succeeded beyond expectations in getting an early strike of excellent coal seams.

We are told that the geological formation has been found to be similar to the Highveld coal-beds of the Transvaal. Inyack Island is a favoured spot, and possesses many natural advantages. It has a high plateau, with plentiful supplies of pure spring water, and is free from fever throughout the year. It has a population of over 400 people, and boasts a little fort manned by a Portuguese garrison. Jutting out as it does into the Indian Ocean, the island has for years been watched with keen curiosity and interest by more than one great European power. With the probability of the discovery of extensive coal deposits, the island becomes of considerable international importance from a strategic point of view.

THE KEY TO SOUTH AFRICA: DELAGOA BAY

In addition to the advantages both to the port and the shipping to be derived from the supply of coal, a good water supply is absolutely necessary. A first-rate supply of good water can now be obtained from the Delagoa Bay Waterworks Company's mains. Piping is laid not only throughout the town in all the principal streets, but is carried right to Reuben Point, so that the inhabitants of that favoured locality can participate in the inestimable benefits conferred by a supply of fresh water laid directly on to their houses. This is a very different state of things from that which prevailed a few years ago, when it was necessary to send one's Kafir boy a long distance for water. The supply, under the circumstances, was of course very meagre, and the boy naturally made it an excuse to stop dawdling about any length of time—for your Kafir dearly loves dawdling, it being one of the few things that he really does to perfection.

Water supply to vessels must help to attract shipping to the port, and now that they can obtain any quantity of good water they would, naturally, put into this port for fresh supplies, which is undoubtedly a very great boon. At present water is taken out to the vessels in lighters, but it will be supplied direct from the mains when the piers and wharves are completed so as to allow ships to come alongside.

Delagoa Bay has felt very severely the recent depression in Johannesburg and the Transvaal, but when the commercial crisis is over, and things boom once again, as they must do ere long, the port will feel the resultant effect, and participate largely in the prosperity.

The greatest desideratum is proper wharfage. It is true that the Portuguese Government has already commenced enormous works, no less than the building of a wharf from the Government Pier right to Reuben Point, over two miles in length. The work, however, has been carried on in a desultory manner, and Heaven only knows when it would be finished if left in the hands of the Portuguese. This is one of the first and most important of the works that it is incumbent upon us to carry through if we obtain control of the Bay.

In a scathing but just criticism on these works, it is stated that "the wharf, when finished, will give the much-needed facilities to shipping and the handling of goods. Of course the building of this wharf has been begun at the wrong end—so characteristic of Portuguese methods. It should have been started from the Customs Pier, and the ground reclaimed to the left of the pier filled in, and used as a dumping wharf for goods. Beyond the Netherlands Pier—the inland side of Lourenço Marques—stores have been run up and the whole appearance of that place altered; further on is the fine Lingham Company Flour Mills, with a capacious granary attached, and some miles up the river the Lingham Timber Company's yards."

It has been urged that Delagoa Bay is too shallow to admit the largest class of steamer. This, however, only refers to certain channels, which are fairly deep as it is, and could very easily be deepened by dredging, so that vessels drawing any depth of water could come right alongside the new wharf when it is built. It is expected that this will be taken in hand if the port is transferred to British control.

The new wharf will prove a wonderful boon to the port; in fact one may safely say that it will be the making of it.

With regard to the land in the rear of the town, reaching back to the foot of the Lebombo Range, many encouraging reports have been circulated. It is stated that the soil is particularly fertile, and that almost anything would be induced to grow; especially is the land suited for the production of mealies, tobacco, vegetables, cereals, and most probably grapes, which latter would promote a splendid industry in the production of native wines. From time to time we receive accounts from different travellers respecting the mineral wealth and agricultural advantages of that little known and less appreciated country of Gazaland. Yet this country is particularly rich in minerals, and is extremely fertile, and only requires to be properly exploited and opened up. Once this has been done it must have a potent effect upon the subsequent prosperity of Delagoa Bay, as the bulk of the produce and consignments, especially of the southern portion of the country, would of course find their way to that fine harbour.

An account recently appeared in the *Bulawayo Chronicle* detailing the experiences of Mr. H. J. Watson during a trip he took to Gazaland for the purpose of studying the character of the country and its agricultural and farming prospects. It states that " Mr. Watson expresses himself as delighted with the country, which he considers the finest, from an agricultural point of view, that he has seen in the whole of South Africa, and in this he agrees with the opinion of many others who know the country. There are already a large number of farmers settled there, both English and Dutch, many of whom possess large herds and flocks of cattle and sheep, which thrive greatly; one farmer alone had 100 calves this season. The soil is exceedingly rich and well adapted for the raising of produce of all kinds, water being plentiful. Some of the farmers have planted out orchards, which in a few years should be bearing abundantly. The three principal drawbacks at present are the locusts, the want of markets, and the labour difficulty. As regards markets, Umtali and, in a less degree, Melsetter, are the only two places where supplies can be disposed of; but that is merely a question of time, as towns are bound to spring up as the country is opened up and railways are laid. In the Sabi district the party came across a number of ancient copper workings, which by analogy to the ancient workings in Matabeleland would point to the fact that the valuable metal could be worked there.

"In the Sabi Valley, near Mafouen's Kraal, some hot springs exist, which appear to possess considerable medicinal properties. The natives both drink from, and bathe in, these springs, which they consider a preventive of fever, and Mr. Watson is of opinion that this idea is a correct one. Although the valley is only about a thousand feet above sea-level, the natives are particularly healthy. The party also crossed the Portuguese border; they found that the Portuguese authorities were giving out farms on practically the same terms as the Chartered

Company. A number of English and Dutch farmers have acquired farms there. The labour difficulty which reigns in Gazaland appears to be the great drawback, the natives being very independent and averse to labour, owing, no doubt, to the ease with which they can live comfortably in that fruitful country without much exertion. A solution no doubt will be found."

With regard to the locust difficulty mentioned, this can, to a very large extent, be neutralised by a recent highly effectual discovery, viz., by inoculation with a particular kind of fungus. Scientific research has been equally as active in this direction as it has been with regard to rinderpest, and there is every reason to hope that with the aid of science we shall soon be able to effectually cope with these and kindred evils, and rise superior to them.

There is a splendid industry for Delagoa Bay, and one that must come in the course of time, viz., sugar-growing. It is announced that a sugar refinery is to be established at Delagoa Bay for the supply of the market there, and in the Transvaal.

The planting of sugar-cane has also been commenced on a property at Infulene. There is no doubt that the sugar-cane would thrive immensely well anywhere in this district, provided that proper attention was paid to its cultivation. Here alone is an immense source of income of a permanent character, and the means of employment of a vast number of people. There is no reason whatsoever why Delagoa Bay and its hinterland should not grow sugar-canes to a very large extent, and successfully compete with the Natal estates. Both the climate and the soil are eminently suited for the cultivation of the sugar-cane, and looking at the fact that Delagoa Bay is so splendidly situated in respect of finding a market for its products to the Transvaal, viâ the railway on the one hand, and a general export trade from the port on the other, there is no cogent reason why this industry should not be a most flourishing and permanent one.

Again, this particular region is well adapted for the supply of grain, the soil being so rich and good and the climate suitable. The whole country around is well supplied with rivers, so that with a certain amount of well-directed labour and expense, the most perfect system of irrigation could be established.

The home demand alone for grain is very great, and this fact—when England rules—should induce farmers to settle here, and make them flourish exceedingly. But further than this, Lourenço Marques could, owing to the cheapness and facilities of transport, successfully compete with other marts.

With all these vast potentialities for successful trade and financial prosperity, Delagoa Bay must of a certainty one day become one of the greatest emporiums and most flourishing ports in the whole continent of Africa. Then there will be work for every one; good, honest, paying work, with substantial fortunes in view.

At the present time, under the Portuguese *régime*, it may well be imagined that there is much want and penury and that work even for the deserving and willing is somewhat difficult to obtain, and for the poor and destitute well-nigh impossible. It was stated recently "that the Portuguese authorities at Lourenço Marques have adopted very stringent measures with regard to destitute aliens. All men out of work, and with no visible means of support, are henceforth to be arrested, and kept to work for six months, and are then to be deported at the colony's expense. Her Majesty's consul at Delagoa sends the following warning: 'This measure will effect most particularly distressed British subjects, of whom there are a considerable number at present in this town. In fact, it is no exaggeration to say that an average of twenty-five per week apply to this consulate for relief. A warning on this subject should be issued in the neighbouring British Colonies.'"

Once England obtains a footing in the Bay this deplorable state of affairs will disappear as if by magic, and a wonderful era of prosperity will be inaugurated. Trade will advance to an extent hitherto undreamed of; the shipping of the port will increase tremendously, agricultural pursuits will flourish, and the town and port will grow and prosper. Already better class buildings are being erected, and the main thoroughfares improved, and the occupation of the Bay by Great Britain would give the necessary impetus to carry on and complete these improvements. With regard to the wonderful advance in the value of land at Lourenço Marques and in the immediate neighbourhood, the statement made in 1898 by M. Nicole—one of the Swiss experts appointed to assess the value of the Delagoa Bay Railway—forms very interesting and instructive reading. He says "that for land in the town as much as £22 has been paid per square metre for building purposes, that land near the station which in 1889 was only worth from one shilling to two shillings per metre was worth in 1898 from ten shillings to two pounds, and that an English company had recently bought land in the town at from £10 to £15 per metre. Still greater had been the advance in value in the outside and residential lands. Thus, one parcel of land consisting of only eight acres, which a few years ago changed hands at £80, was sold in 1896 to some financiers, hailing from Johannesburg, for £30,000.

This is all the more wonderful when it is considered that the land was nothing but bare sand, without any improvements whatever."

The value of land, it will be seen, has increased by leaps and bounds, and would undoubtedly have shown even greater advances if the Portuguese had effected the necessary improvements to the harbour and town. Of recent years they have done something, it is true, but any one who knows the dilatory nature of the Portuguese colonial officials and their woful lack of energy will not be surprised that comparatively little remedial work has been effected.

In 1897 it was reported from Lourenço Marques that authority had been received from the Portuguese Government for the expenditure of £1,000,000 upon improvements to the Delagoa Bay harbour. The scheme, which was sanctioned by the Lisbon Parliament, was a very extensive one, and comprised the building of quays, landing-places, and other harbour works, as well as the improvement of the town, drainage works, &c.

Once Great Britain obtained control over this magnificent natural harbour, she would directly put in hand and expeditiously carry out those very necessary works which were only in contemplation by the Portuguese.

A good trade will, no doubt, be done in the importation of frozen meat, which is now allowed to enter the province. In fact a concession relating to this has been granted by the municipality.

The Natalians have been very successful in the production of excellent tea, which is not so astringent as the Indian and China teas, it having a less percentage of tannin in it, but has a delicate flavour. Tea-growing might be commenced tentatively in the rich country behind Delagoa Bay, and if found to answer, as there is every chance of its doing, it would add another important industry to the long list that will be formed and prove flourishing in the future. In the same way experiments should be made in the cultivation of coffee, tobacco, &c., for if soil, facilities for irrigation, and climate go for anything, this country should become the most productive in South Africa, especially when we consider the situation and the splendid facilities for transport.

There have recently been some very important discoveries of petroleum about sixty miles from Lourenço Marques, and prospecting parties have been sent out. If the mineral exists in any quantity these discoveries should prove most valuable.

There are a number of mealie mills and also saw mills in Lourenço Marques, and a good flour mill at Matolla. These are all flourishing and do very good business, as does the distillery erected at the border town of Ressano Garcia.

To conclude, there has been a new and most important innovation in the export of bar gold from Johannesburg, *viâ* Lourenço Marques. Mr. Consul A. C. Ross says, in the consular report for 1898, that it is an entirely new departure in local trade, and that this first shipment consisted of £260,000 worth of gold. It was made by the French South African Bank to Paris; the inclusive freight charged from Lourenço Marques to Paris was ¾ per cent., and the journey occupied thirty days.

If it were not for the fact that we hope to acquire possession of Delagoa Bay and the railway before long, this new departure might prove very serious to us in the future.

With regard to dynamite, a correspondent of the *Cape Times* recently wrote as follows: " Whilst the attention of the world is directed to Transvaal affairs in general, and the dynamite monopoly in particular, it is not known that another dynamite concession is in existence within an easy distance of Pretoria.

" Mousinho Albuquerque, in his capacity as Royal Commissioner of Portuguese East Africa, just two years back granted four Portuguese residents of Delagoa Bay a concession to manufacture dynamite and all other kinds of explosives within the district of Delagoa Bay. This concession has been signed by the King of Portugal.

" Fortunately for the Transvaal mining industry this infant prodigy forced into existence has failed in obtaining a foster-father such as its brother in Pretoria. Meanwhile the Delagoa Bay Dynamite Concession has life, but not having any influential sponsors it has received very little attention since its birth. The concession does not rank in Lourenço Marques as a corner-stone of independence, nor is it a subject which has claimed the notice of the press, capitalists, or governments.

" The concession embraces the sole right of manufacturing all explosives for a period of nineteen and a half years. A lease of two hundred hectares, equal to five hundred acres, on any site selected by the concessionaires in any part of the district of Delagoa Bay, and the right to construct a branch line to connect the factory with the trunk line to Johannesburg. On the expiration of the lease for nineteen and a half years the Portuguese Government agree to take over all the works at a valuation, or re-let the same on lease for a further term of not less than nineteen and a half years. By a Portuguese-Transvaal treaty, duly recognised, the produce of Mozambique enters the Transvaal free of duty, and is carried over the Delagoa Bay-Pretoria Railway at about one-third rates.

"Comparisons, we are taught, are odious, but those appertaining to the Transvaal and Delagoa Bay history assist our attempts at gaining knowledge. The Pretoria dynamite concession, well advanced in years, is worth a fabulous sum, but under the exploitation of its strange godfathers it may endanger the independence of the greatest gold-producing country in the world. On the other hand, the Delagoa Bay dynamite concession remains an empty, valueless offspring of Portuguese blundering, yet it is a priceless instrument, which, if it were in the hands of some, could be utilised to checkmate Kruger and his Hollander parasites more than all the mistakes and hesitating diplomacy of later years."

CHAPTER VII

POLITICAL HISTORY

THE Portuguese having discovered Delagoa Bay and formed the small station, which they named after the explorer, Lourenço Marques, remained content for a very long period with the bare honour of the discovery and made very little attempt at establishing either " an effective occupation " or a trade with the natives.

Up to the beginning of the seventeenth century they did a little trading in the purchase of ivory, sending a small vessel round the coast to the Bay at very long intervals, but eventually they ceased even to do that, although both the English and the Dutch did some trading there.

A Dutch expedition landed and formed a

small settlement in 1721, on the site of the present town of Lourenço Marques, they having taken possession of the place, which they found uninhabited. They only retained possession for a few years, however, as it proved too unhealthy for them, owing to the prevalence of malarial fever. All around the settlement were large swamps, where the fever microbes flourished, and it is no wonder that they quickly decimated the ranks of the unlucky expedition.

An Austrian expedition, which, however, was under the command of an Englishman, established a trading station and erected a fort in 1776, but were, a few years afterwards, expelled by the Portuguese, and their building was destroyed.

In 1787 the Portuguese built a fort and trading station, which were afterwards destroyed by the French.

In 1822 Captain Owen conducted an expedition to Delagoa Bay for the purpose of making a complete survey of the place. He obtained the sanction of the Portuguese Government, as the expedition was formed entirely in the interests of geography and science, and the Government, moreover, gave directions requiring the coast officials to assist and protect the members of the expedition. Having arrived at Delagoa Bay, Captain Owen was informed by the Portuguese that they had no control over the native chiefs, and that they were *in no way subject to Portuguese rule*, and consequently they could afford him no protection.

The party then commenced their explorations, following the course of the Tembe river. They fell in with a number of the natives, together with their chief, a man named Mazeta. This chief ardently desired to come under English rule, and therefore approached Captain Owen on the subject, who agreed to the cession on behalf of Great Britain. A document was then prepared, dated the 8th of March, 1823, signed by the chief and duly witnessed, by which he ceded the whole of the country under his control to Great Britain. Later on another chief, named Makasuni, whose country extended from the sea to the Maputa river, and who also wished to come under English rule, signed a document, dated the 23rd of August, 1823, placing his tribe and the whole of his territory under the protection of Great Britain. No sooner, however, had the English expedition departed than the Portuguese approached these chiefs and forced them to sign documents declaring that they were, and always had been, subject solely to Portuguese rule. For many years the whole of the country remained in a most unsettled state, there being frequent risings and terrible fights among the various native tribes. The Portuguese were totally powerless to quell these risings, and in point of fact had absolutely no control whatsoever over the natives. The native chiefs did not recognise Portuguese rule and openly flouted their authority.

In the year 1852 the "policy of dismemberment" was inaugurated by the Sand River Convention, and in 1854 Great Britain acknowledged the Independence of the Orange Free State. At the same time the great value and importance of Delagoa Bay was not lost sight of by England, and consequently in 1861, when H.M.S. *Nar-*

cissus visited those waters, her commander caused the British flag to be hoisted and the territory proclaimed British.

The Portuguese Government at once raised an outcry and strongly protested against these steps, while urging her own claim to the whole of the country. Nothing of very great importance, however, occurred until the year 1869, when Portugal entered into a commercial treaty with the South African Republic, and by it defined the boundary lines. This treaty had the effect of awakening the British Government from its torpor, and at once a claim was made on the strength of the documents that Captain Owen had obtained from the native chiefs in 1823. This claim the Portuguese utterly repudiated.

At this time England had an unexampled opportunity of acquiring Delagoa Bay by purchase. The High Commissioner repeatedly warned Lord Kimberley of its immense strategic and commercial importance and the necessity of its acquisition by Great Britain. The time was propitious, as Portugal was in her usual needy state, and, moreover, had not become alive to the fact that in a few short years the harbour, which has rightly been called the " Key to South Africa," would grow most enormously in value and become a port of the first importance. Incredible as it seems to us at the present day, Lord Kimberley let slip this magnificent opportunity of acquiring the Bay when, it is said, it might have been purchased for the paltry sum of about £12,000. Instead of this he elected to go to arbitration, and thus this one glorious opportunity was gone for ever. It was a political error of the gravest importance, for what then was a mere question of thousands as the purchase-price is now represented by millions.

In 1872, by a protocol signed at Lisbon, the dispute was submitted to the arbitration of Marshal Macmahon, the President of the French Republic. After the case had been argued on both sides—well argued and carefully prepared on the part of the Portuguese and carelessly so by the English —the President, on the 24th of July, 1875, gave his award in favour of Portugal.

He decided that the want of effective occupation on the part of Portugal did not vitiate her claims, and actually awarded her more territory than she had asked for. He gave to the Portuguese the whole of the land, including Lourenço Marques and Delagoa Bay, down to lat. 26° 30′ S., and running inland from the sea to the Lebombo Mountains.

Before this award was given, viz., on the 17th of June, 1875, the Portuguese Government bound themselves " not to cede or sell to any third Power the territories on the South-East Coast of Africa awarded to Portugal by the decision of the President of the French Republic, without having previously given Her Britannic Majesty's Government the opportunity of making a reasonable offer for the purchase or acquisition, by other arrangements satisfactory to Portugal, of the territory thus awarded."

In the year 1891 this pledge was repeated and confirmed by a treaty negotiated by Lord Salisbury, and was made to extend to the whole of the Portuguese territories to the south of the Zambesi. This Anglo-

Portuguese Convention was signed at Lisbon on the 11th of June, 1891, and by one of the Articles it was provided that "the two Powers agree that in the event of one of them proposing to part with any of the territories to the south of the Zambesi assigned by these Articles to their respective spheres of influence, the other shall be recognised as possessing a preferential right to the territories in question, or any portion of them, upon terms similar to those proposed."

It is only of recent years that Portugal seems to have awakened to the fact that Delagoa Bay is a magnificent harbour and a truly valuable possession. England slept; a lethargy crept over the Imperialists, and the Colonial Office was calmly indifferent.

However, when trouble with the Transvaal arose, attention was immediately drawn to the Bay, and it was clearly seen what a menace and grave danger it would prove if it fell into the hands of an enemy. Not only would our shipping be imperilled, but the port itself would be used for the purpose of landing troops and importing supplies.

How real this danger was may be seen at a glance when it is remembered that during the friction with the Boers at the close of 1895, Germany tried to land troops there for service in the Transvaal, absolutely ignoring England, the paramount Power.

On the 3rd of January, 1896, the German Emperor sent his cablegram congratulating President Kruger after the defeat of Dr. Jameson's troops at the battle of Doornkop, and this was directly after followed by the commissioning of the Particular Service Squadron.

It will thus be seen that it is of the utmost importance, in the interests of Great Britain, that we should acquire possession of the Bay. This fact is brought home to us more strongly when we remember that the neighbouring island of Madagascar is in the hands of the French, who have fortified it and made it a strong naval station. French activity has been very marked of recent years, and it is easy to see that, having done us out of Madagascar, they are particularly anxious to safeguard that possession and obtain complete control over the Mozambique Channel. While Delagoa Bay remained in the hands of Portugal France felt herself fairly safe, as that country could not harm her, and, above all, the mere fact of occupation meant that the other Powers were kept out.

The moment, however, that negotiations for the cession of the Bay to England were opened, France felt what a menace it might prove to her possession, and that if the cession became a *fait accompli*, her grand scheme of complete control of the Mozambique Channel would melt into thin air. France then strained every nerve to put a spoke in England's wheel. Her great desire was to obtain the internationalisation of the waters of the Bay, so that England should never have a chance of exercising her right of pre-emption in the very probable event of Portugal electing to sell owing to her financial difficulties.

It was precisely these financial difficulties that brought about the *rapprochement* between England and Portugal. The Portuguese are indebted to us in a very large amount, apart from the award of the arbitrators in connection with the Delagoa Bay Railway, and this, taken in conjunction with the fact that their internal affairs are in a most deplorable state, induced the Government of Portugal to approach us. It is absolutely necessary for Portugal's well-being that she should raise considerable loans for the purpose of getting rid of her most pressing liabilities.

In the Peninsular War England rendered yeoman service to Portugal. In 1811 the British Parliament granted the sufferers by war in Portugal £100,000. We befriended Portugal throughout the war, our army, under Wellington, being everywhere successful. Portugal thus became our debtor for some millions of pounds sterling.

In the summer of 1898 negotiations between England and Germany were entered into with the result that an agreement was arranged referring to English and German interests in Africa. This agreement dealt in particular with Portuguese territory south of the Zambesi, including Delagoa Bay. It is easy to understand that certain sections of the German public, egged on by the

Anglophobe organs of the Press, protested strongly against their Government entering into an *entente cordiale* with Great Britain. Consequently vigorous efforts were made to justify the departure of the German Government from its attitude as defined by the late Foreign Secretary, Baron Marschall von Bieberstein, in his despatch of 1st February, 1895. The despatch declared " that the material interests which Germany had created by the construction of railways and the establishment of commercial relations with the Transvaal required the maintenance of the Transvaal as an independent State." The Government organs in Berlin stated that the "material interests" to which Baron Marschall von Bieberstein referred might be safeguarded in a variety of ways, and that opinions as to the best manner of maintaining them might change in accordance with circumstances. The German Government thus attuned the public mind to the fact that Delagoa Bay was to pass into the hands of Great Britain, while special clauses in the agreement favours both Powers regarding the ultimate division of Portuguese territory in South Africa.

In precisely the same way the Portuguese Government sought to allay the feelings of the excitable Portuguese subjects. But for the strong opposition made by the people, Delagoa Bay would have passed into English hands some years previously. The outcry raised by the Communists was so great, however, that the Government was overruled, and the negotiations fell through for the time being.

It can easily be imagined that so staunch an Imperialist as the Founder of Rhodesia, with his grand schemes for the expansion of the Empire, would direct his attention to this most important harbour. As a fact, Mr. Cecil Rhodes has been untiring in his exertions for many years past, to obtain an interest in Delagoa Bay as well as in the railway. This astute and far-seeing politician readily recognised the vast importance both commercially and strategically of the Bay, and realised what a menace it would prove to British interests if it fell into the hands of a foreign Power. Consequently he

THE KEY TO SOUTH AFRICA: DELAGOA BAY

has for long past schemed and used his best endeavours to place Delagoa Bay under British rule.

Had he been in power when Lord Kimberley had his unrivalled opportunity of purchasing the Bay, that magnificent harbour would have passed into our hands immediately. At that time, however, Cecil Rhodes had neither won wealth nor power, although he was working hard at the diamond fields with a stern resolve and a fixed purpose to acquire both, so that he might place himself in a position to properly serve the country he loves so well.

His great ambition has always been the expansion of the Empire and the furtherance of the true interests of the great British realm. But for him that magnificent territory of Rhodesia would have been lost to England, and but for his splendid example and untiring patriotic work, England's paramountcy in South Africa would have been seriously jeopardised.

Mr. Rhodes readily foresaw that Delagoa Bay meant more to us than to any other nation, and hence his continued and laudable efforts to secure it.

POLITICAL HISTORY

Mr. Chamberlain again, unlike some of his predecessors in office, has always been fully aware of the vast importance of the Bay and of its acquisition by Great Britain.

Mr. Chamberlain's task has been no easy one; the position has materially altered of late years, for the place has grown greatly in value and importance, and it is now a most valuable asset to any country. Moreover, a Colonial Secretary is to a certain extent fenced in and hemmed around, and he requires to be a very strong man to break through the bonds. To both Mr. Rhodes and Mr. Chamberlain is due a very large meed of praise as well as gratitude from every Englishman who has at heart his country's honour, welfare, and glory.

The Colony of Mozambique, which was founded in 1508, is an eloquent example of the Portuguese colonial policy, which is simply a woful mixture of apathy, crass ignorance, and culpable neglect. From its inception the colony has showed a yearly loss, which has proved a heavy drain on Portugal, until in 1893, when there was a small balance on the right side. Considering the immense wealth and great potentialities of the country, it really amounts to a sin that this state of things should be allowed to exist, for surely there is a strong moral obligation resting on the country under whose ægis a land is placed to properly develop and colonise it. The magnificent natural resources of this fertile land have been allowed to remain undeveloped, and it is now well time that a country capable and willing to undertake the task should obtain possession of the land.

It undoubtedly devolves upon Great Britain, as the supreme Power, to effect this, as she is admittedly the greatest colonising power in the world, and has, moreover, unlimited resources. Quite apart, however, from the great advantages that the country itself would derive from a change of ownership, and the protection that would be afforded if it was placed under the ægis of the British flag, a further and equally important point would be gained, viz., that we should be a step nearer the goal of South African federation. The greater our sphere of influence and the more preponderating our interests in South Africa, the better chance we have of more quickly attaining the much-desired union, which is bound to come, and is merely a question of time.

Colonial federation is the panacea for all international jealousies and disagreements and racial strife. When this eventuates some of the gravest difficulties and dangers that now confront our politicians will be solved.

It is only natural that the great Imperialist, Mr. Rhodes, should strive might and main to accomplish this great end. In a famous speech he made at Salisbury in September, 1897, he said that his whole future should be directed to the unity of the various South African States, and that his future policy would be clear and open to that end. In the following year, speaking at Cape Town in support of the Progressive candidates for the Legislative Council, he spoke of the inconsistencies of the general tactics followed by the Afrikander Bond, and charged its organ, the *Ons Land*, with fostering race hatred and obstructing the attainment of a united South Africa. He maintained that there was a bond of union between the citizens of South Africa, who must, he said, by the ties of kinship ever remain one and indivisible, whether they resided in Cape Colony, Natal, the Transvaal, or in far Rhodesia. This union he believed would eventually prevail, and in conclusion declared that what he desired was a closer union between the Colonies, and in his opinion such a union was perfectly possible of attainment during the next five years.

Mr. Rhodes is an ardent champion of federation, for he plainly sees, as every right-thinking Englishman must, that without consolidation there can be no solidarity, and the Empire would be in grave peril of disintegration.

On the subject of Imperial policy, the following excerpt from Mr. Chamberlain's speech delivered recently in Birmingham, clearly shows our Colonial Secretary's views. He said: "I do not argue for Empire simply because it contributes to the material interests of the United Kingdom. It does that no doubt, and the result in not unimportant when we consider what the existence of the United Kingdom means in the civilisation of the world. But it does much more. It constitutes part of the discipline of our nation which has made us great, for we have found in the fulfilment of our duty to our dependencies an escape from provincial narrowness and selfish isolation. It is this policy which has developed the national character, and I firmly believe that in spite of many faults by which it has been accompanied, in spite even of the crimes which are sometimes laid to its charge, it has made on the whole for peace and good government, and for the happiness of countless millions of the human race."

True Imperialists have none of the Jingo element about them which the " Little Englander body" indiscriminately ascribes to them. Quite apart from their presumed insatiable desire for the acquisition of fresh territory, they have one guiding star, which is the consolidation of the Empire. For the purpose of achieving this laudable object it is often absolutely necessary that some small tract of country or some port be acquired, and this for the preservation of our possessions as a whole, for the furtherance of trade, as a precautionary measure against those nations who are only too anxious to disturb the balance of power, and—as a most important corollary—for the maintenance of peace. No stronger exemplification of this praiseworthy procedure for the solidarity of our Colonial possessions and the consolidation of the Empire could possibly be sought than in the endeavour by Great Britain to secure the possession of Delagoa Bay. All the benefits specified would accrue to our beloved Empire, and, further, the best interests of the present owners, the Portuguese, would also be served; for they would be relieved of an incubus, and at the same time find a happy solution for their financial difficulties.

The possession of Delagoa Bay by Great Britain would go a long way to clear the political atmosphere, and would, moreover, firmly establish our position as the supreme Power in South Africa.

BOOKS FOR RECREATION AND STUDY

PUBLISHED BY
T. FISHER UNWIN,
11, PATERNOSTER
BUILDINGS, LON-
DON, E.C. ....

T. FISHER UNWIN, Publisher,

MR. MAGNUS

BY

F. REGINALD STATHAM

Second Edition. Crown 8vo., cloth, **6s.**

Some Press Opinions on the First Edition.

"One of the most powerful and vividly written novels of the day."—*Nottingham Guardian.*
"A grim, terrible, and convincing picture."—*New Age.*
"Very impressive."—*Saturday Review.*
"Distinctly readable."—*Speaker.*   "A remarkable book."
"Full of incident."—*Liverpool Mercury.*   [*Standard.*
"One of the most important and timely books ever written."
        Newcastle Daily Mercury.
"A vivid and stirring narrative."—*Globe.*
"An exceedingly clever and remarkable production."—*World.*
"A book to be read."—*Newsagent.*
"A terrible picture."—*Sheffield Independent.*
"One of the best stories lately published."—*Echo.*
"Worth reading."—*Guardian.*   "A sprightly book."—*Punch.*
"The story is very much brought up to date."—*Times.*
"Vivid and convincing."—*Daily Chronicle.*
"The story is good and well told."—*Pall Mall Gazette.*
"Ought to be immensely popular."—*Reynolds' Weekly Newspaper.*
"A most readable story."—*Glasgow Herald.*
"A brilliant piece of work."—*Daily Telegraph.*
"The story should make its mark."—*Bookseller.*
"Admirably written."—*Sheffield Daily Telegraph.*
"The more widely it is read the better."—*Manchester Guardian.*
"Will find many appreciative readers."—*Aberdeen Free Press.*
"Exciting reading."—*Daily Mail.*
"Can be heartily recommended."—*Lloyd's Weekly Newspaper.*
"A well-written and capable story."—*People.*
"Well written."—*Literary World.*

11, Paternoster Buildings, London, E.C.

T. FISHER UNWIN, Publisher,

TROOPER PETER HALKET OF MASHONALAND

BY

OLIVE SCHREINER

Author of "Dreams,"
"Real Life and Dream Life," &c.

Crown 8vo., cloth, **2s. 6d.**

" We advise our readers to purchase and read Olive Schreiner's new book 'Trooper Peter Halket of Mashonaland.' Miss Schreiner is one of the few magicians of modern English literature, and she has used the great moral, as well as the great literary, force of her style to great effect."—*Daily Chronicle.*

" The story is one that is certain to be widely read, and it is well that it should be so, especially at this moment; it grips the heart and haunts the imagination. To have written such a book is to render a supreme service, for it is as well to know what the rough work means of subjugating inferior races."—*Daily News.*

" Some of the imaginative passages are very fine. . . . The book is powerfully written."—*Scotsman.*

" Is well and impressively written."—*Pall Mall Gazette.*

11, Paternoster Buildings, London, E.C.   *p*

T. FISHER UNWIN, Publisher,

SOME 3/6 NOVELS

Uniform Edition of MARK RUTHERFORD'S works. Edited by REUBEN SHAPCOTT. Crown 8vo., cloth.

The Autobiography of Mark Rutherford. Fifth Edition.

Mark Rutherford's Deliverance. New Edition.

Miriam's Schooling, and other Papers. By MARK RUTHERFORD. With Frontispiece by WALTER CRANE. Second Edition.

The Revolution in Tanner's Lane.

Catharine Furze: A Novel. By MARK RUTHERFORD. Fourth Edition.

Clara Hopgood. By MARK RUTHERFORD.

"These writings are certainly not to be lightly dismissed, bearing as they do the impress of a mind which, although limited in range and sympathies, is decidedly original."—*Times.*

The Statement of Stella Maberly. By F. ANSTEY, Author of "Vice Versâ." Crown 8vo, cloth.
"It is certainly a strange and striking story."—*Athenæum.*

Silent Gods and Sun-Steeped Lands. By R. W. FRAZER. Second Edition. With 4 full-page Illustrations by A. D. MCCORMICK and a Photogravure Frontispiece. Small crown 8vo., cloth.
"Mr. Frazer writes powerfully and well, and seems to have an intimate acquaintance with the sun-steeped land, and the strange beings who people it."—*Glasgow Herald.*

Paul Heinsius. By CORA LYSTER. Crown 8vo., cloth.
"This is an extremely clever and altogether admirable, but not altogether unkindly, anatomisation of Teutonic character."—*Daily Chronicle.*

My Bagdad. By ELLIOTT DICKSON. Illustrated. 8vo., cloth.
"Related with a refreshing simplicity that is certain to approve itself to readers."—*Bookseller.*

Silk of the Kine. By L. MCMANUS (C. MacGuire), Author of "Amabel: A Military Romance." Crown 8vo., cloth.
"We have read 'The Silk of the Kine,' from the first page to the last, without missing a single word, and we sighed regretfully when Mr. McManus brought the adventures of Margery MacGuire and Piers Ottley to a close."—*Literary World.*

A Pot of Honey. By SUSAN CHRISTIAN. Crown 8vo., cloth.
"The book is the outcome of a clever mind."—*Athenæum.*

Liza of Lambeth. By W. SOMERSET MAUGHAM. Crown 8vo., cloth.
"An interesting story of life and character in the Surrey-side slums, presented with a great deal of sympathetic humour."—*Daily Chronicle.*

11, Paternoster Buildings, London, E.C.

T. FISHER UNWIN, Publisher,

THE HALF-CROWN SERIES

❖ ❖ ❖

Each Demy 12mo., cloth.

1. **A Gender in Satan.** By RITA.
2. **The Making of Mary.** By JEAN M. MCILWRAITH.
3. **Diana's Hunting.** By ROBERT BUCHANAN.
4. **Sir Quixote of the Moors.** By JOHN BUCHAN.
5. **Dreams.** By OLIVE SCHREINER.
6. **The Honour of the Flag.** By CLARK RUSSELL.
7. **Le Selve.** By OUIDA. 2nd Edition.
8. **An Altruist.** By OUIDA. 2nd Edition.

THE CAMEO SERIES

❖ ❖ ❖

Demy 12mo., half-bound, paper boards, price **3s. 6d.**
Vols. 14-17, **3s. 6d.** *net.*
Also, an Edition de Luxe, limited to 30 copies, printed on Japan paper. Prices on application.

1. **The Lady from the Sea.** By HENRIK IBSEN. Translated by ELEANOR MARX AVELING. Second Edition. Portrait.
4. **Iphigenia in Delphi,** with some Translations from the Greek. By RICHARD GARNETT, LL.D. Frontispiece.
5. **Mireio:** A Provençal Poem. By FREDERIC MISTRAL. Translated by H. W. PRESTON. Frontispiece by JOSEPH PENNELL.
6. **Lyrics.** Selected from the Works of A. MARY F. ROBINSON (Mme. JAMES DARMESTETER). Frontispiece.
7. **A Minor Poet.** By AMY LEVY. With Portrait. Second Edition.
8. **Concerning Cats:** A Book of Verses by many Authors. Edited by GRAHAM R. THOMSON. Illustrated.
9. **A Chaplet from the Greek Anthology.** By RICHARD GARNETT, LL.D.
11. **The Love Songs of Robert Burns.** Selected and Edited, with Introduction, by Sir GEORGE DOUGLAS, Bart. With Front. Portrait.
12. **Love Songs of Ireland.** Collected and Edited by KATHERINE TYNAN.
13. **Retrospect, and other Poems.** By A. MARY F. ROBINSON (Mme. DARMESTETER), Author of "An Italian Garden," &c.
14. **Brand:** A Dramatic Poem. By HENRIK IBSEN. Translated by F. EDMUND GARRETT.
15. **The Son of Don Juan.** By Don José ECHEGARAY. Translated into English, with biographical introduction, by JAMES GRAHAM. With Etched Portrait of the Author by Don B. MAURA.
16. **Mariana.** By Don José ECHEGARAY. Translated into English by JAMES GRAHAM. With a Photogravure of a recent Portrait of the Author.
17. **Fiamma Vestalis,** and other Poems. By EUGENE MASON. Frontispiece after Sir EDWARD BURNE-JONES.

T. FISHER UNWIN, Publisher,

THE MERMAID SERIES

The Best Plays of the Old Dramatists.
Literal Reproductions of the Old Text.

Post 8vo., each Volume containing about 500 pages, and an etched Frontispiece, cloth, **3s. 6d.** *each.*

1. **The Best Plays of Christopher Marlowe.** Edited by HAVELOCK ELLIS, and containing a General Introduction to the Series by JOHN ADDINGTON SYMONDS.

2. **The Best Plays of Thomas Otway.** Introduction by the Hon. RODEN NOEL.

3. **The Best Plays of John Ford.**—Edited by HAVELOCK ELLIS.

4 and 5. **The Best Plays of Thomas Massinger.** Essay and Notes by ARTHUR SYMONS.

6. **The Best Plays of Thomas Heywood.** Edited by A. W. VERITY. Introduction by J. A. SYMONDS.

7. **The Complete Plays of William Wycherley.** Edited by W. C. WARD.

8. **Nero,** and other Plays. Edited by H. P. HORNE, ARTHUR SYMONS, A. W. VERITY, and H. ELLIS.

9 and 10. **The Best Plays of Beaumont and Fletcher.** Introduction by J. ST. LOE STRACHEY.

11. **The Complete Plays of William Congreve.** Edited by ALEX. C. EWALD.

12. **The Best Plays of Webster and Tourneur.** Introduction by JOHN ADDINGTON SYMONDS.

13 and 14. **The Best Plays of Thomas Middleton.** Introduction by ALGERNON CHARLES SWINBURNE.

15. **The Best Plays of James Shirley.** Introduction by EDMUND GOSSE.

16. **The Best Plays of Thomas Dekker.** Notes by ERNEST RHYS.

17, 19, and 20. **The Best Plays of Ben Jonson.** Vol. I. edited, with Introduction and Notes, by BRINSLEY NICHOLSON and C. H. HERFORD.

18. **The Complete Plays of Richard Steele.** Edited, with Introduction and Notes, by G. A. AITKEN.

21. **The Best Plays of George Chapman.** Edited by WILLIAM LYON PHELPS, Instructor of English Literature at Yale College.

22. **The Select Plays of Sir John Vanbrugh.** Edited, with an Introduction and Notes, by A. E. H. SWAEN.

PRESS OPINIONS.

"Even the professed scholar with a good library at his command will find some texts here not otherwise easily accessible; while the humbler student of slender resources, who knows the bitterness of not being able to possess himself of the treasure stored in expensive folios or quartos long out of print, will assuredly rise up and thank Mr. Unwin."—*St. James's Gazette.*

"Resumed under good auspices."—*Saturday Review.*

"The issue is as good as it could be."—*British Weekly.*

"At once scholarly and interesting."—*Leeds Mercury.*

11, Paternoster Buildings, London, E.C.

T. FISHER UNWIN, Publisher,

THE STORY OF THE NATIONS

A SERIES OF POPULAR HISTORIES.

Each Volume is furnished with Maps, Illustrations, and Index. Large Crown 8vo., fancy cloth, gold lettered, or Library Edition, dark cloth, burnished red top, **5s.** *each.—Or may be had in half Persian, cloth sides, gilt tops; Price on Application.*

1. **Rome.** By ARTHUR GILMAN, M.A.
2. **The Jews.** By Professor J. K. HOSMER.
3. **Germany.** By the Rev. S. BARING-GOULD.
4. **Carthage.** By Professor ALFRED J. CHURCH.
5. **Alexander's Empire.** By Prof. J. P. MAHAFFY.
6. **The Moors in Spain.** By STANLEY LANE-POOLE.
7. **Ancient Egypt.** By Prof. GEORGE RAWLINSON.
8. **Hungary.** By Prof. ARMINIUS VAMBERY.
9. **The Saracens.** By ARTHUR GILMAN, M.A.
10. **Ireland.** By the Hon. EMILY LAWLESS.
11. **Chaldea.** By ZENAIDE A. RAGOZIN.
12. **The Goths.** By HENRY BRADLEY.
13. **Assyria.** By ZENAIDE A. RAGOZIN.
14. **Turkey.** By STANLEY LANE-POOLE.
15. **Holland.** By Professor J. E. THOROLD ROGERS.
16. **Mediæval France.** By GUSTAVE MASSON.
17. **Persia.** By S. G. W. BENJAMIN.
18. **Phœnicia.** By Prof. GEORGE RAWLINSON.
19. **Media.** By ZENAIDE A. RAGOZIN.
20. **The Hansa Towns.** By HELEN ZIMMERN.
21. **Early Britain.** By Professor ALFRED J. CHURCH.
22. **The Barbary Corsairs.** By STANLEY LANE-POOLE.
23. **Russia.** By W. R. MORFILL.
24. **The Jews under the Roman Empire.** By W. D. MORRISON.
25. **Scotland.** By JOHN MACKINTOSH, LL.D.
26. **Switzerland.** By R. STEAD and LINA HUG.
27. **Mexico.** By SUSAN HALE.
28. **Portugal.** By H. MORSE STEPHENS.
29. **The Normans.** By SARAH ORNE JEWETT.
30. **The Byzantine Empire.** By C. W. C. OMAN, M.A.
31. **Sicily: Phœnician, Greek and Roman.** By the late E. A. FREEMAN.
32. **The Tuscan and Genoa Republics.** By BELLA DUFFY.
33. **Poland.** By W. R. MORFILL.
34. **Parthia.** By Prof. GEORGE RAWLINSON.
35. **The Australian Commonwealth.** By GREVILLE TREGARTHEN.
36. **Spain.** By H. E. WATTS.
37. **Japan.** By DAVID MURRAY, Ph.D.
38. **South Africa.** By GEORGE M. THEAL.
39. **Venice.** By the Hon. ALETHEA WIEL.
40. **The Crusades:** The Latin Kingdom of Jerusalem. By T. A. ARCHER and CHARLES L. KINGSFORD.
41. **Vedic India.** By ZENAIDE A. RAGOZIN.
42. **The West Indies and the Spanish Main.** By JAMES RODWAY, F.L.S.
43. **Bohemia.** By C. E. MAURICE.
44. **The Balkans.** By W. MILLER.
45. **Canada.** By Dr. BOURINOT.
46. **British India.** By R. W. FRAZER, LL.B.
47. **Modern France.** By ANDRÉ LE BON.
    The Franks. By LEWIS SERGEANT, B.A.
49. **Austria.** By SIDNEY WHITMAN.
50. **Modern England before the Reform Bill.** By JUSTIN MCCARTHY, M.P.
51. **China.** By Professor DOUGLAS.

11, Paternoster Buildings, London, E.C

T. FISHER UNWIN, Publisher,

THE CHILDREN'S STUDY
● ● ●

Long 8vo., cloth, gilt top, with photogravure frontispiece, price **2/6** *each.*

Scotland. By Mrs. OLIPHANT.
Ireland. Edited by BARRY O'BRIEN.
England. By FRANCES E. COOKE.
Germany. By KATE FREILIGRATH KROEKER, Author of "Fairy Tales from Brentano," &c.
Old Tales from Greece. By ALICE ZIMMERN.
France. By MARY ROWSELL.
Spain. By LEONARD WILLIAMS.
Rome. By MARY FORD.
Canada. By J. R. McILWRAITH.

OPINIONS OF THE PRESS ON "SCOTLAND."

"For children of the right age this is an excellent little history."—*Daily News.*
"Enough of fault-finding with a writer who has otherwise performed his task in a perfectly charming manner."—*Daily Chronicle.*
"The best book for the rising Caledonian that has appeared for many a day."
"Simple, picturesque, and well-proportioned."—*Glasgow Herald.* [*Scotsman.*
"A charming book full of life and colour."—*Speaker.*
"As a stimulator of the imagination and intelligence, it is a long way ahead of many books in use in some schools."—*Sketch.*
"The book is attractively produced. Mrs. Oliphant has performed her difficult task well."—*Educational Times.*
"A work which may claim its place upon the shelves of the young people's library, where it may prove of not a little service also to their elders."—*School Board Chronicle.*

OPINIONS OF THE PRESS ON "IRELAND."

"Many who are children no longer will be glad of this compact but able introduction to the story of Ireland's woes. The form of the volume is particularly attractive."
British Weekly.
"We heartily congratulate Mr. Barry O'Brien upon this interesting little volume. The style is intensely interesting."—*Schoolmaster.*
"It is well that the youth of England, who have entered into a serious inheritance and who will soon be the voters of England, should have some conception of the country with whom they are so closely bound up, and for whose past their fathers are so heavily responsible. We do not know of any work so fitting for imparting to them this knowledge as the present, which, therefore, we heartily commend to all teachers as the best text-book of Irish history for the young."—*Daily Chronicle.*

OPINIONS OF THE PRESS ON "ENGLAND."

"Terse, vivid, well-informed."—*Speaker.*
"Pleasantly written, and well within the capacity of a young child. ... We anticipate with pleasure the appearance of the succeeding volumes of 'The Children's Study.'"—*School Guardian.*
"Admirably done .... always easy of understanding."—*Scotsman.*

OPINIONS OF THE PRESS ON "GERMANY."

"We have seldom seen a small history so well balanced, and consequently so adequate as an introduction to the subject."—*Educational Times.*
"Painstaking and well written."—*Daily Chronicle.*
"Clear as accurate. It is just the sort of book to give to a youngster who has to study Teutonic history."—*Black and White.*
"An interesting historical series."—*Pall Mall Gazette.*

11, Paternoster Buildings, London, E.C.

T. FISHER UNWIN, Publisher,

BUILDERS OF GREATER BRITAIN

EDITED BY

H. F. WILSON

A Set of 10 *Volumes, each with Photogravure Frontispiece, and Map, large crown* 8vo., *cloth,* 5s. *each.*

The completion of the Sixtieth year of the Queen's reign will be the occasion of much retrospect and review, in the course of which the great men who, under the auspices of Her Majesty and her predecessors, have helped to make the British Empire what it is to-day, will naturally be brought to mind. Hence the idea of the present series. These biographies, concise but full, popular but authoritative, have been designed with the view of giving in each case an adequate picture of the builder in relation to his work.

The series will be under the general editorship of Mr. H. F. Wilson, formerly Fellow of Trinity College, Cambridge, and now private secretary to the Right Hon. J. Chamberlain at the Colonial Office. Each volume will be placed in competent hands, and will contain the best portrait obtainable of its subject, and a map showing his special contribution to the Imperial edifice. The first to appear will be a Life of Sir Walter Ralegh, by Major Hume, the learned author of "The Year after the Armada." Others in contemplation will deal with the Cabots, the quarter-centenary of whose sailing from Bristol is has recently been celebrated in that city, as well as in Canada and Newfoundland; Sir Thomas Maitland, the "King Tom" of the Mediterranean; Rajah Brooke, Sir Stamford Raffles, Lord Clive, Edward Gibbon Wakefield, Zachary Macaulay, &c., &c.

The Series has taken for its motto the Miltonic prayer:—

"*Thou Who of Thy free grace didst build up this Brittannick Empire to a glorious and enviable height. With all her Daughter Islands about her, stay us in this felicitie.*"

1. **SIR WALTER RALEGH.** By MARTIN A. S. HUME, Author of "The Courtships of Queen Elizabeth," &c.

2. **SIR THOMAS MAITLAND;** the Mastery of the Mediterranean. By WALTER FREWEN LORD.

3. **JOHN CABOT AND HIS SONS;** the Discovery of North America. By C. RAYMOND BEAZLEY, M.A.

4. **EDWARD GIBBON WAKEFIELD;** the Colonisation of South Australia and New Zealand. By R. GARNETT, C.B., L.L.D.

5. **LORD CLIVE;** the Foundation of British Rule in India. By Sir A. J. ARBUTHNOT, K.C.S.I., C.I.E.

   RAJAH BROOKE; the Englishman as Ruler of an Eastern State. By Sir SPENSER ST. JOHN, G.C.M.G

   ADMIRAL PHILIP; the Founding of New South Wales. By LOUIS BECKE and WALTER JEFFERY.

   SIR STAMFORD RAFFLES; England in the Far East. By the Editor.

T. FISHER UNWIN, Publisher,

THE ADVENTURE SERIES
POPULAR RE-ISSUE.

Each large crown 8vo., fully illustrated. Popular re-issue, **3s. 6d.** *per vol. ; in two styles of binding, viz., decorative cover, cut edges ; and plain library style, untouched edges.*

1. **Adventures of a Younger Son.** By EDWARD J. TRELAWNEY. Introduction by EDWARD GARNETT.
2. **Madagascar;** or, Robert Drury's Journal during his Captivity on that Island. Preface and Notes by Captain S. P. OLIVER, R.A.
3. **Memoirs of the Extraordinary Military** Career of John Shipp.
4. **The Buccaneers and Marooners of** America. Edited and Illustrated by HOWARD PYLE.
5. **The Log of a Jack Tar:** Being the Life of James Choyce, Master Mariner. Edited by Commander V. LOVETT CAMERON.
6. **Ferdinand Mendez Pinto, the Portu**guese Adventurer. New Edition. Annotated by Prof. A. VAMBÉRY.
7. **Adventures of a Blockade Runner.** By WILLIAM WATSON. Illustrated by ARTHUR BYNG, R.N.
8. **The Life and Adventures of James** Beckwourth. Mountaineer, Scout, Pioneer, and Chief of Crow Nation Indians. Edited by CHAS. G. LELAND.
9. **A Particular Account of the European** Military Adventurers of Hindustan. Compiled by HENRY COMPTON.

11, Paternoster Buildings, London, E.C.

T. FISHER UNWIN, Publisher,

MASTERS OF MEDICINE

EDITED BY

ERNEST HART, D.C.L.,

Editor of "The British Medical Journal."

Large crown 8vo., cloth, **3s. 6d.** *each.*

Medical discoveries more directly concern the well-being and happiness of the human race than any victories of science. They appeal to one of the primary instincts of human nature, that of self-preservation. The importance of health as the most valuable of our national assets is coming to be more and more recognised, and the place of the doctor in Society and in the State is becoming one of steadily increasing prominence ; indeed, Mr. Gladstone said not many years ago that the time would surely come when the medical profession would take precedence of all the others in authority as well as in dignity. The development of medicine from an empiric art to an exact science is one of the most important and also one of the most interesting chapters in the history of civilisation. The histories of medicine which exist are for the most part only fitted for the intellectual digestion of Dryasdust and his congeners. Of the men who made the discoveries which have saved incalculable numbers of human lives, and which have lengthened the span of human existence, there is often no record at all accessible to the general reader. Yet the story of these men's lives, of their struggles and of their triumphs, is not only interesting, but in the highest degree stimulating and educative. Many of them could have said with literal truth what Sir Thomas Browne said figuratively, that their lives were a romance. Hitherto there have been no accounts of the lives of medical discoverers in a form at once convenient and uniform, and sold at a popular price. The "Masters of Medicine" is a series of biographies written by "eminent hands" intended to supply this want. It is intended that the man shall be depicted as he moved and lived and had his being, and that the scope and gist of his work, as well as the steps by which he reached his results, shall be set forth in a clear, readable style.

The following is a condensed list of some of the earlier volumes :—

AUTHOR.	TITLE.
STEPHEN PAGET	*John Hunter*
D'ARCY POWER	*William Harvey*
H. LAING GORDON	*Sir James Simpson*
JOHN G. MCKENDRICK	*Hermann von Helmholtz*
SIR WILLIAM STOKES	*William Stokes*
MICHAEL FOSTER	*Claude Bernard*
TIMOTHY HOLMES	*Sir Benjamin Brodie*
J. F. PAYNE	*Thomas Sydenham*
C. L. TAYLOR	*Vesalius*

11, Paternoster Buildings, London, E.C.

T. FISHER UNWIN, Publisher,

WORKS BY MARTIN A. S. HUME

F.R.H.S., Editor of the "Calendar of Spanish State Papers of Elizabeth" (Public Record Office).

THE COURTSHIPS OF QUEEN ELIZABETH

With Portraits

Fourth Edition. Large crown 8vo., cloth, **6s.**

"It is undeniably an important addition to the history of the Elizabethan period, and it will rank as the foremost authority on the most interesting aspect of the character of the Tudor Queen."—*Pall Mall Gazette.*
"A clear and very interesting account. An excellent book."—*Times.*
"A connected and consistent, though assuredly a most extraordinary, story. . . . A fascinating picture."—*Standard.*
"A delightful book."—*Daily Telegraph.*

THE YEAR AFTER THE ARMADA

AND OTHER HISTORICAL STUDIES

Second Edition. Illustrated. Demy 8vo., cloth gilt, **12s.**

"A most valuable and conscientiously written historical work."—*Spectator.*
"The whole book is extremely interesting, and at once instructive and amusing."—*Speaker.*
"Deserves a wide circulation, and we trust that a proper reward will follow close upon its merits."—*Literary World.*
"Major Hume has thrown the most curious and valuable light on the Armada period. Full of delightful sketches of men and things."—W. L. COURTNEY in *The Daily Telegraph.*
"A work which adds many a fresh page to English, and one may say to European history. . . . From first to last the volume is excellent reading, while the entertaining style in which the matter is presented and the undeniable authority of the writer . . . render the book of special interest and permanent value."—*The Morning Post.*
"Quite as good as a novel—and a good deal better, too. The book is so bright and vivid that readers with the common dislike of history may venture on its pages unafraid."—ANDREW LANG in *Cosmopolis.*

SIR WALTER RALEGH

Being Vol. I. of the series entitled "Builders of Greater Britain," each vol. with photogravure frontispiece and map.

Large crown 8vo., cloth, **5s.** *each.*

"There is not a dull page in it, and, with his skilful telling of it, the story of Raleigh's life and of his times reads like a romance."—*Pall Mall Gazette.*

11, Paternoster Buildings, London, E.C.

T. FISHER UNWIN, Publisher,

SOME WORKS BY REV. E. J. HARDY

"The Murray of Matrimony, the Baedeker of Bliss."

HOW TO BE HAPPY THOUGH MARRIED

Popular Edition, gilt edges, cloth, bevelled boards, **3s. 6d.**
Presentation Edition, white vellum, cloth, levelled boards, gilt edges, in box, **7s. 6d.**

"An entertaining volume. . . . The new guide to matrimonial felicity.—*Standard.*
"This charming volume. . . . Wit and wisdom abound in its pages; as for the good stories, they are almost too plentiful."—*Spectator.*

Uniform in style and prices with the foregoing.

THE FIVE TALENTS OF WOMAN
A Book for Girls and Young Women

THE BUSINESS OF LIFE
A Book for Everyone

Square imperial 16mo., cloth, **3s. 6d.**—*Presentation Edition, bevelled boards, gilt edges, in box, **7s. 6d.***

"Calculated to teach the art of happiness and contentment as well as mere exhortation can teach it."—*Times.*
"Pleasant as well as profitable reading."—*Literary World.*
"A host of social subjects are treated in a way at once wise and witty, and in a manner as delightful to read as they are pleasantly 'improving.'"—*Daily Telegraph.*

THE SUNNY DAYS OF YOUTH
A Book for Boys and Young Men

Square Imperial 16mo., cloth, **3s. 6d.**—*Presentation Edition, elegantly bound, bevelled boards, gilt edges, **7s. 6d.***

"It is an excellent book for a serious-minded boy."—*Scotsman.*
"The pleasantest reading possible . . . this useful little book."—*Educational Review.*
"As well written as it is unquestionably well-intentioned."—*Leeds Mercury.*

FAINT YET PURSUING
Square Imperial 16mo. Popular Edition. Crown 8vo., cloth, **3s. 6d.**

"Will meet with an extensive recognition."—*Morning Post.*
"Short and sensible . . . they form fresh and breezy reading."—*Glasgow Herald.*

"MANNERS MAKYTH MAN"

Presentation Edition, imperial 16mo., cloth, bevelled boards, in box, **7s. 6d.**; cloth, **6s.** Popular Edition, small square 8vo.; cloth, **3s. 6d.**

"Good-natured, wholesome, and straightforward."—*Saturday Review.*
"A really delightful volume, well adapted for family reading."—*Christian World.*

THE LOVE AFFAIRS OF SOME FAMOUS MEN
Imperial 16mo., cloth, **3s. 6d.**

11, Paternoster Buildings, London, E.C.

T. FISHER UNWIN, Publisher,

WORKS BY PROF. PASQUALE VILLARI

THE LIFE AND TIMES OF GIROLAMO SAVONAROLA

Translated by LINDA VILLARI

*New and Cheaper Edition in one volume. Fully Illustrated.
Cloth, large crown,* **7s. 6d.**

" No more interesting book has been issued during the present season."
Pall Mall Gazette.
"The most interesting religious biography that we know of in modern times."
Spectator.
" A book which is not likely to be forgotten."—*Athenæum.*
" By far the best book on Savonarola available for English readers."—*Standard.*
" Is perhaps *the* book of the publishing season."—*Star.*
"Sincere, complete, and, upon the whole, well-balanced and candid."—*Yorkshire Post.*
" A work of very great value."—*Scotsman.*
" No more graphic view of the ecclesiastical and social life of ancient Italy has been opened up for us than this of Linda Villari."—*Morning Leader.*
"As complete and trustworthy as care, judgment, and the fullest investigation can make it."—*Dundee Advertiser.*
" A credit to the publisher."—*Independent.*

THE LIFE AND TIMES OF NICCOLÒ MACHIAVELLI

*New and Cheaper Edition. Fully Illustrated. Large crown 8vo.,
cloth,* **7s. 6d.**

"Indispensable to the serious student of Machiavelli, his teaching and his times."
Times.
"The fullest and most authoritative history of Machiavelli and his times ever given to the British public."—*Glasgow Herald.*
" May be regarded as an authority on the times of which it treats. . . . The book is enriched with rare and interesting illustrations, and with some valuable historical documents."—*Daily Telegraph.*

BY FRANK HORRIDGE

LIVES OF GREAT ITALIANS

Illustrated. Large crown 8vo., cloth, **7s. 6d.**

Opinions of the Press.

" A poetical, romantic, and charmingly written book, which will be popular with all who love their Italy."—DOUGLAS SLADEN in *Literary World.*
" Able, eloquent, and interesting."—*Queen.*

11, Paternoster Buildings, London, E.C.

T. FISHER UNWIN, Publisher,

THE CENTURY DICTIONARY

Six volumes bound in cloth, gilt lettered, sprinkled edges,
per vol. **£2 2s.**
Do. in half morocco, marbled edges, per vol. **£2 16s.**
BOOKCASE for holding the Dictionary, price **£3 3s.**

Size of each volume 13 in. × 9½ in. × 2¼ in.

PRESS NOTICES.

"The exceptional merits of the 'Century Dictionary' are beyond dispute."—*Times.*

"One of the most notable monuments of the philological industry of the age."
Daily Telegraph.

"It is a work of great ability, fine scholarship, and patient research in many widely different departments of learning."—*Standard.*

"As we turn the leaves of this splendid work, we feel acutely the inadequacy of any description apart from actual handling of the volumes."—*Daily Chronicle.*

"It is fuller, more complete, with fewer faults than any rival."—*Pall Mall Gazette.*

THE CYCLOPÆDIA OF NAMES

Cloth, **£2 2s.** *net.; half morocco,* **£2 15s.** *net.*

Size—13 in. × 9½ × 2¼ in.

PRESS NOTICES.

"A book of ready reference for proper names of every conceivable kind."—*Daily News.*

"The 'Cyclopædia of Names' deserves to rank with important works of reference, for though its facts on any given subject are, of course, elementary, they can be quickly found, and, on the whole, they are admirably chosen."—*Standard.*

"A most handsome and solid volume . . . . It will be found exceedingly useful. . . . It is beautifully printed."—*Daily Chronicle.*

"A most valuable compilation, and one which will be valued for the great mass of information which it contains."—*Glasgow Herald.*

"Every library of reference, no matter how richly stocked, will be the richer for having it . . . . may be consulted freely without the inconveniences of human haulage."—*Scotsman.*

11, Paternoster Buildings, London, E.C.

CUBA AND PORTO RICO
WITH THE OTHER ISLANDS OF
THE WEST INDIES,
BY ROBERT T. HILL,
Of the United States Geological Survey.

BAHAMAS,
JAMAICA,
HAITI,
SAN DOMINGO,
ST. THOMAS,
ST. KITTS,
ANTIGUA,
MONTSERRAT,
GUADELOUPE,
MARTINIQUE,
ST. LUCIA,
BARBADOS,
ST. VINCENT,
GRENADA,
TRINIDAD.

A valuable Work of Reference.
A Scientific Presentation.
An indispensable Guide.
A readable Narrative.
500 Pages.
160 Illustrations.
Price 16s.

Flora,
Climate,
Soil,
Products,
Minerals,
Agriculture,
Scenery,
Topography,
Sanitation,
People,
Transportation,
Statistics,
History,
Routes of travel,
Administration,
Accessibility,
Possibilities.

"His book is a very good example of its kind, carefully written, full of the information that is required."—*The Times.*

"He has written the most important book that has been published on the subject."—*Chicago Tribune.*

"His volume of 429 pages, with profuse Illustrations and an index, forms a little condensed library of reference."—*N. Y. Times.*

"The book is well and ably written ... is brightened by a truly magnificent series of photographs ... beautifully reproduced on fine paper."—*Edinburgh Scotsman.*

Tourists to Cuba, Porto Rico and the West Indies will find this most reliable and the only General Handbook.

T. FISHER UNWIN, PATERNOSTER SQUARE, LONDON

www.ingramcontent.com/pod-product-compliance
Lightning Source LLC
Chambersburg PA
CBHW020859230426
43666CB00008B/1238